Praise for *Hol*

"Art Kehler's stories about small town Montana are not just hilarious, they capture the best and worst of the spirit of a very complicated place. This collection takes you right down Main Street." — Russell Rowland, author of *Fifty-Six Counties: A Montana Journey, In Open Places, The Watershed Years, High and Inside,* and more

"After several years of gentle persuasion (aka "nagging") I'm very pleased that Art Kehler has finally put a collection of his wonderful essays together. From the first time I heard him read one of his works I was impressed by his writing, beautiful imagery, and self-deprecating sense of humor.

Art is a gifted story-teller. Whether he's writing of snake hunting, adventures in the Tri-cities, or making improvements to the English language, one finds in each story his wit, humor, and—just a wee bit beneath the surface—a gem of wisdom. I suspect Art's hesitation in bringing this work together may have been some combination of his genuine modesty and his earnest, painstaking quest for perfection. I think you'll agree that *Hollowtop Smoke Signals* was worth the wait.— Gary R. Forney, author of *Thomas Francis Meagher: Irish Rebel, American Yankee, Montana Pioneer; Discovery Men; Dawn in El Dorado: The Early Mining Camps and Settlement of the Montana Territory;* and *It Takes All Kinds: Stories from Virginia City,* and more

"Sometimes, it seems the so-called civilized world is flying off the rails and half it's people gone crazy. Those times, it feels great to live in the country, where it's easy to forget the high-speed craziness of big cities and the problems plaguing the world.

"For anyone suffering from the tribulations about global calamities, or for anyone who just wants to feel good, I've found the perfect prescription. It's Art Kehler's *Hollowtop Smoke Signals: a collection of Humorous Essays....* "Art's essays take you down home to the 'tri-cities' of Harrison, Pony and Norris, Montana, (combined populations,382), where he describes the charms, challenges and various misadventures of living in such a rustic but beautiful place nestled on the northeastern fringe of the Tobacco Root Mountains....

"Art's essays include a harrowing tale of a climb to the top of Hollowtop Mountain, for which the book is named. Stop worrying, relax and pick up Art's book. You'll get lots of laughs and that's the best medicine you can find." — Geoff Hamill, editor of the Madisonian, Ennis, MT.

"In one of the resonant essays of humorist and thinker, Art Kehler, there is a quote describing discussion of small town traditions and citizens. 'I know you, you're one of us.' Readers of the delightful *Hollowtop Smoke Signals,* be they rural or urban, will indeed be 'one' with this corner of Montana (the Tri-Cities of Harrison, Pony, and Norris—total population less than 400), the place, and the people. Along the way, life's quirks, pleasures, and perils, as well as some hidden gems of beautiful descriptions of Montana, are told in witty, entertaining, and often insightful writing. In the tradition of Mark Twain, James Thurber, Bill Bryson, and Garrison Keillor, Montana has it's own chronicler: Art Kehler. Great reading!" — Marcia Melton, author of *The Boarding House*, *Joe Henry's Journey* and more

Hollowtop Smoke Signals

A Collection of Humorous Essays

Art Kehler

Hollowtop Smoke Signals

ISBN: 978-1-937849-47-4

Raven Publishing, Inc.
P.O. Box 2866
Norris, MT 59745
www.ravenpublishing.net

Printed in the United States of America

Library of Congress Cataloging in Publication Control Number: 2017059498

To my late father: Bill Kehler Sr.,
whose spontaneous wit and love of
language inspired me to write.

TABLE OF CONTENTS

Tri-city Tales

Outdoor Misadventures

The Art of Aging Gracelessly

Blasts From The Past

Technology Challenged

Random Ruminations

Harrison, Montana – population 137

Pony, Montana – population 118

TRI-CITY TALES

Norris, Montana – population 137

Learning the Lingo

The struggles of adapting to a new dialect

I first arrived in Montana, while on vacation with my family, when I was seven-years-old. Even at that tender age, I sensed that someday I would return here to stay. After three return trips, over fourteen years, my dream of living in Montana became a reality. Due to having moved before, I was fully aware "fitting-in" at a new location is not always easy. Nevertheless, overall, the friendly Tri-cities' (Harrison, Pony and Norris) citizens amiably accepted the alien in their midst. However, there was one aspect of my personality that clearly did not fit in—my "Pennsylvania brogue."

For a while, it seemed my every utterance was grounds for hilarity. However, in fairness, it did take me quite a while to get over my deeze, doze, dats and dems. For some reason, the term, "youz guys," invariably resulted in guffaws and finger-pointing. Additionally, my tortured mispronunciations of such in-state designations as Missoula, Axalotl Lakes, and Absaroka had residents rolling on the ground, with their feet twitching and mouths agape.

Also my witty, back-east expressions were not always well received. For instance, the proprietor of Harrison's, long-defunct, Duffy's Tavern did not relish having his place of business referred to as "Da Joint." As well, a devoted tavern patron, who periodically burst into spontaneous song, expressed grievous displeasure when I opined that he "sounded like a constipated screech owl." Further, it was brought to my attention that, when greeting an area resident, the proper term was "Howdy,'" not "Yo," I was also curtly informed that area students, upon graduating from high school, received a "diploma" rather than a "pardon from the governor."

Locals couldn't understand why I struggled with the words "barrow pit" and "coulee" when, not only had I never before heard either term, but I also didn't have the slightest idea what they were. Furthermore, I must admit the mixed-drink term, "whiskey ditch," did not stir me to salivation.

Despite the many humbling setbacks, I was determined to fit-in. Hence, for endless hours, I sat in front of a mirror and practiced my Montana dialect. Rehearsing the regional syllable emphasis of individual words proved helpful. I even added nasal tone as needed. I studied the hand gestures that accompanied certain words and phrases. Diligently, I mimicked the tongue, lip, eyeball, and eyebrow contortions used by residents while they bloviated. Despite the excruciating nightly facial muscle cramps, I soldiered on.

Over time, my linguistic blunders became fewer and fewer until, thankfully, my manner of speech began to be regarded as intelligible. To my dismay, townsfolk actually started to seek me out for serious conversation. Finally, I had managed to fully fit-in.

Yet, to this day, people sometimes ask, "How did you end up in Montana?" My immediate response is an outright denial of the unfounded rumor that I was "thrown out of Pennsylvania." Though I don't recall hysterical mobs pleading with me not to leave, the truth is I left (albeit in the middle of the night) of my own free will. After that crucial clarification, I mention, "Pop liked to fish."

Overall, I lived back east for the first twenty-one years of my life. For the succeeding forty-five years, I have chosen to live in the great state of Montana. I have never returned to my birth state, not even to visit relatives. That fact sums up my feelings about Montana better than anything I could say. In the final analysis, "learning the lingo" proved to be well worth the ego-bruising effort.

One-sided Town

A unique place to call home

Behold, the 21st century is upon us. It is a period of burgeoning human population. There are 7.5 billion humans on planet earth and over 300 million people in the United States. Merging metropolises stretch from Massachusetts to Maryland. Yet, despite the surging hordes, I find myself living in a "one-sided town."

What is a one-sided town? It is a village that lies wholly on one side of the chief boulevard. In this instance, the entire population (all 137 souls) resides east of the paved primary road. The west side of said road consists of open pasture. The urban area extends for approximately twelve blocks and averages three blocks wide. The only sidewalks line the east side of the main street and there are no stoplights.

Sadly, I have heard my beloved settlement referred to in such unflattering terms as, "nondescript," "blink and you'll miss it," "two feet from the end of the world," etc. Strangers ask, "Why would anyone want to live here?" Obviously they are unaware of the advantages of life in a single-sided community.

To begin, our hamlet's telephone listings comprise a grand total of four pages. As a result, it takes longer to locate the listings in the regional phone book than it takes to find and dial the number. Truth be known, one needs only to shout in order to orally contact a goodly portion of the population. Therefore some citizens spurn the use of telephones for local calls in favor of the time honored "backyard bellow." This admittedly archaic practice nonetheless provides more expedient information transfer than that found in more extensive communities.

Moreover, single-sided township driving standards are a bit more liberal than those in rambling communities. For instance, since my whole village lies on one side of the main street, deciding which direction cars traversing said road will turn, shouldn't be cause for lengthy deliberation. As a result, local logic disdains the use of turn signals, reckoning brake lights are sufficient warning of an impending turn.

Similarly, because of the compactness of my single-sided outpost, side streets are of limited length. Furthermore, given that all of the side roads are dirt, obviously there are no painted divider lines. As such, directional lanes are subject to individual interpretation.

These factors have given birth to a locally cherished motoring maneuver dubbed the "stubby street u-ey." To perform a stubby street u-ey, a driver, without slowing, abruptly steers into whichever side of the unpaved road appears least likely to loosen the fillings of the teeth. Then, he or she executes a rousing 180-degree curve, to advance in the opposite direction. This utilitarian maneuver permits seamless traffic flow with a minimum of cumbersome legalities. Clearly, the stubby street u-ey is seldom available to city residents, oppressed as they are by myriad traffic lanes.

Regrettably, some visitors are unaware of our driving customs. As a result, more than a few have pasted lips to their windshields. Thankfully, one-sided townsfolk are a forgiving lot, not likely to hold rancor against those unfamiliar with our quaint traditions.

Additionally, tobacco chewers are especially blessed to live in my single-sided burgh. While traversing the main drag, they are free to spew westward with abandon. Of course the old rule of, "check the wind direction first," still applies.

A further example of solitary-sided settlement uniqueness

involves our dogs undergoing reverse evolution. Because my community is too small to warrant fire hydrants, its young male dogs suffer a growth phase of mass confusion. Fortunately, older dogs school them in the use of historically regressive utilities to facilitate their essential urges such as flagpoles, fence posts, and idle pant legs. Not surprisingly, locals pay close attention to sniffing dogs.

It has been said that it is in the "little things" of life that we find our truest joy. Sole-sided villages are fertile grounds in which to savor those very things. I refer to such little things as beginning each day with an unhindered view of 10,604-foot Hollowtop Mountain. Also, judiciously spaced streetlights afford undiminished observation of the night sky, beneath which coyotes often yip at the moon. As well, abandoned homesteads border the community, where footprints of the past lie scarcely beneath the loam. Most importantly, there are the friendly, unpretentious folks who call this humble hamlet home.

As can be seen, there are many sides to my one-sided town that those traveling through never encounter. It is by reason of those little things, which defy measure, that I consider myself singularly fortunate to make my home in Harrison, Montana, U.S.A.

Harrison's Covert Constituents

A novel idea for increasing a village's population

Recently, while in Bozeman, I was asked where I live. I responded that I lived in Harrison. The response was pretty much what I have come to expect: "Where's Harrison?" I then asked if this person had ever been to Pony. His response was a cheerful, "Sure." I then explained that one cannot reach the paved road to Pony from Bozeman without going through Harrison first. Upon reflection, he acknowledged having passed through a spattering of buildings before turning onto the road to Pony. Regrettably, this sad story is too often a reflection of current perception. Like it or not, my beloved town is in danger of being overlooked to oblivion.

Obviously, Harrison's recognition problems are centered on our paltry population. As such, increasing the town's human population would seem the simplest solution. However, such action fails to recognize our fiercely independent townsfolk that already consider the settlement to be intolerably overpopulated. Clearly, the solution called for some "out of the box" thinking.

After mining the depths of my fertile mind, I recalled that our municipal area contains a sizable number of wild critters. Our furry neighbors have chosen to take up residence in our yards, raise their families among us, and make their living here. There is even evidence that our native brethren have formed a rudimentary "neighborhood watch" program. As a case in point, recently a local woman, while perched on the commode, observed a bull moose peering through her bathroom window to check on her well being. With that endearing act of neighborliness in mind, the answer to Harrison's problem seemed obvious—Why not register our town's resident deer and moose as voters?

By enacting my daring plan, we could nearly double our number of registered voters while, at the same time maintaining our human citizens' treasured personal space. Most importantly, our newfound citizens would provide Harrison with increased political clout. Of course, a modest ploy of pen would be required so as not to alarm county and state officials. Therefore, appropriate names and addresses for our covert constituents would need to be configured. Following is my suggested initial list:

- Blarney O'Rutagain - Seasonal Drive
- Alvin Applemuncher - Orchid Alley
- Buck Barkscrapper - Ivory Lane
- Jane Doe - Anonymous Avenue
- Spike Van Horn - Antler Hollow
- Calamity Clovenhoof – Clodhopper Cliffs
- Rocky Rackstag – Trophy Trail
- Toots Cudchomper–Green Acres
- Winnie Whitetail – Fantail Road
- Petunia Pietaster–Window Sill Stroll
- Last but not least there's our aforementioned moose, Bullwinkle Von Megasnoz, who resides pretty much where he darn well pleases.

Further, legitimate-sounding occupations would also need to be identified for our new citizens. Following is a compilation of plausible occupations:

- Bullwinkle's Fence Stretching
- Eco-Friendly Lawn Maintenance
- Swollen Neck Reproductive Clinic

- Automobile Brake Testers
- Hat Racks Are Us
- Sharp Ears Hearing Center
- Fender Bender Arts & Crafts
- Ungulates Unlimited Political Action Committee

As demonstrated, with a little creative endeavor, I believe Harrison may well regain its luster of yore as the "Queen City of Central, South Willow Creek." Let's see out-of-towners ignore that.

Pony Pete, Prairie Prognosticator

A western view of Groundhog Day

On Feb 2nd, I was driving west on the road between Harrison and Pony, Montana. Just as the car's radio reminded me that this day was "Groundhog Day," I glanced out the driver's side window and saw my first gopher of the year. I pulled off the road to savor the occasion. As I watched the gopher, the broadcaster mentioned "Punxsutawney Phil," the Pennsylvania groundhog for whom, supposedly, the holiday was named.

Waxing poetic, the commentator went on to repeat the legend of the exalted groundhog: if he were to emerge from his burrow and see his shadow, six more weeks of winter awaited. On the other paw, if old Phil didn't see his shadow, spring would come early. Such is his legendary stature that Keystone State folks proudly proclaim Punxsutawney Phil as the "world's most famous prognostic rodent." While listening, I wondered how the unheralded, western, prognostic rodent outside my car compared. Then, as though reading my thoughts, the announcer went on to reveal some little known facts about Phil.

To begin, his full name was unveiled as, Punxsutawney Phil Sowerby. Now I could grasp him having a title reflecting his region. Additionally, pets customarily have a first name—but a last name? Really! That sounded pretty pompous to me. I wasn't buying that until presented with a legal birth certificate and an ancestory.com-approved family history.

Next, the radio reporter testified that Punxsutawney Phil didn't really "emerge" on February 2nd. Rather, he was dragged from a cage and hustled off to nearby Gobbler's Knob, where he was rudely dumped into a man-dug burrow. After all the assorted dignitaries and media folks arrived, the hapless woodchuck was again yanked from his temporary quarters. From there, Phil predicted the coming of spring—while having no idea where he was.

Lastly, the broadcaster said that, shortly after his sage prediction, pampered Phil would be put back into the cage and returned to his "real" home—beneath the town library. There, he and his wife, Phyllis, would be doted on by two handlers until next year's ballyhooed prediction. Based on those shocking revelations, I thought perhaps a more fitting name for Punxsutawney Phil's holiday would be "Househog Day."

Unable to bear anymore, I dubbed the nearby gopher, "Pony Pete, Prairie Prognosticator." No one had to drag our local rodent out of his burrow (let alone a cage), while still snoring. Pony Pete emerged of his own will because he was powerful hungry. By so doing, like a hairy robin, the Prairie Prognosticator predicted spring would come when it was danged well ready—and that was enough. Only a dummy would predict the end of Montana's winter.

Suddenly, a streaking blur descended from the sky. Aghast, I watched as a hawk snatched Pony Pete from atop his prairie home. The image of that pitiless predator, winging off with the prophetic rodent dangling from its claws, was indeed a grim sight. Unlike his eastern counterpart, there were no handlers, dignitaries, and reporters to protect our Prairie Prognosticator. But then, fiercely independent westerner that he was, Pony Pete wouldn't have had it any other way.

Finally, in profound sadness, I drove on to Pony, and

recounted the story of Pony Pete. Soon, it was the "talk of the town"—even bigger news than calf scours. Since, there has been speculation about erecting a "Pony Pete, Prairie Prognosticator" statue in the Pony Park and of an annual February 2nd celebration of his brief but inspiring life. Take heed Punxsutawney Phil Sowerby.

Full-Fledged Feud

The saga of a man and a cantankerous canine

Overall, I've gotten along well with dogs over the years. One might even say I have a way with them. Still, years ago, there was one particularly cantankerous canine with which I seemed destined to cross fangs. He belonged to a revered village elder that lived up the street from me in Harrison. The dog's lineage was best described as a "son of a thousand fathers" breed. In regard to his appearance, suffice it to say he had to sneak up on a mud puddle to get a drink. Perhaps that's why the perpetually angry critter trounced every canine in town. Except for his owner, nobody in Harrison was able to befriend him. Still, the old gentleman loved his furry pal and wouldn't think of chaining him. So, the dog began charging my car.

Initially, I felt sorry for the unfortunate creature. So, one day, I tossed a treat out of my car's window while passing his abode. To my dismay, the agile animal swallowed it in mid charge. Then, without missing a step, he surged upward to offer me an intimate view of his fangs, tongue, and tonsils, along with a whiff of foul breath. For the next week, my peace offerings were, likewise, rudely engulfed. Clearly, such tactless ingratitude could not go unanswered.

From then on, every day, as I drove home, the possessed beast would dash out into the street in its usual rage. And just as surely, every day, I would spew coffee out the window on his head. After a while, it got to be a tradition between us. I think he even acquired a taste for caffeine. Once, while passing his house, my hairy antagonist was nowhere to be seen. I stopped the car and waited. Still no dog. Finally, I blew the horn. Plainly embarrassed at having been caught asleep on the job, the irate hound sprinted from behind his house barking furiously. Satisfied, I spurted coffee out the window on his head and drove home. We both felt better.

Finally, on a rainy day, my fondest hopes came true. As usual, the manic mongrel streaked toward my vehicle with his great, gaping yap fully unhinged. Then, just as he arrived at my car, the front tire struck a mud puddle. Ecstatically, I watched as dirty water gushed down his throat, surged up his nostrils and blew under his eyelids. The drenched mutt hacked so violently that all four feet came off the ground. Hence, the self-anointed monarch of Madison Street lost face in front of the entire neighborhood. It was wonderful.

Though I didn't think it possible, after that, his charges became even more ferocious. Additionally, as opposed to the previous direct assaults, my adversary began charging from different angles. Thus, I was compelled to disgorge at matching angles, which resulted in splattered coffee stains inside my automobile. Right then and there, the situation degraded to a full-fledged feud. Still, there was no denying, the dog was crafty.

Some time later, the old gentleman sadly informed me that his furry pal had unexpectedly died of natural causes. With hanky unfurled, I dabbed my eyes and feigned suitable grief. Yet, deep down, I knew that I (the supposedly more intelligent species) had allowed raw emotion to triumph over my better nature. So, in grudging respect, for a week after his demise, I continued to spew coffee out the car's window when driving past his former lair. The feud was over, and I had to admit, I kinda-sorta missed the cantankerous canine.

Covert Resource

Exposing a deliberate exclusion

Surely Southwestern Montana is a place of impressive natural resources. One has only to page through State-published tourism brochures to see them heralded: towering mountains, vast prairies, plentiful wildlife, etc. Nevertheless, one natural resource, of which this state has aplenty, seems conspicuously absent from the above-mentioned pamphlets. I refer, in particular, to our invigorating winds. Obviously, omitting reference to something so much a part of life in Montana, smacks of deliberate exclusion. As such, I feel duty-bound to share with those considering moving here, some bluster-coping tactics I have mastered during four decades living in "The Big Sky Country."

To begin, the wind blows here the year round. That's not to say that there are never any calm days. During the warmer months especially, there are significant periods of comparative tranquility. Yet, over the span of a year, such times are outnumbered by days when the currents roar.

On countless occasions, I have observed newcomers exit their dwellings with perfectly coifed locks, only to be struck by a lurking surge of air. Instantly, the poor miserable wretches appear to have combed their hair with a hand grenade. On especially blustery days, even bald men look disheveled, as conspicuous, wave-like ruffles radiate across their naked pates. It soon becomes obvious why hats are an essential part of the Montana ensemble. Indeed, it is the first piece of apparel many natives don while dressing for the day. For immigrants, I advocate purchasing a tight-fitting hat, preferably one with a chinstrap that fastens using a mini chain tightener.

Likewise, another hazard concerns the act of hanging laundry on the line to dry. At any time of the year, the use of contemporary clothespins is risky. I dare say having to borrow the neighbor's ladder, in order to retrieve your Fruit of the Looms from his roof, is an indignity that no mortal should suffer. Additionally, this awkward mishap is invariably accompanied by disparaging remarks of a deeply personal nature. Hence, I strongly recommend the use of vice grips to hang clothes outside.

As a rule, the Montana wind saves its most exemplary efforts for winter. It is then, when combined with frigid temperatures, snow, and the occasional airborne cow pie, that people get to savor wind at its best. But, take heart. In the days immediately following a blizzard, the gale dosage often decreases dramatically. Coincidentally, the temperature commonly drops far below zero. Naturally, even a hint of breeze exacerbates the cold exponentially. During such days, a piping hot latte will metamorphose into a frozen brick—whilst steam still wafts from the lid. Under such immoderate chill factors, my advice to unseasoned residents is simple, "Beginning with quality buffalo-hide long johns, apply consecutive layers of clothing until comfortably warm. Then—don't leave the house."

Above all, the most critical skill recent inhabitants must learn is the art of traversing icy streets. Frequently, when crossing a thoroughfare, a person suddenly finds his or her feet zipping smartly over the slippery surface, at the mercy of a relentless wind. At such times, I have found it helpful to drop into a squat akin to that of a Japanese sumo wrestler. Firmly slapping both feet onto the slick pavement, while hunkering into that widespread, low-hung stance greatly reduces the chances of being blown off one's pins.

Furthermore, this sturdy posture provides a modest mode of navigation. If for instance, one desires to veer left to avoid an oncoming truck, one merely slides the left foot forward. Then by canting the toes of said foot inward and twisting the upper-body leftward, one can not only evade the vehicle but also glide to within a couple of hundred yards of where the person hoped to arrive. As for braking, the sumo pose offers little. The only effective stopping methodologies I have found are the time-honored "face and butt plants." Of course, such maneuverings are likely to draw stares, but as the old adage proclaims, "Pride goeth before the fall."

In closing, let me be the first to offer my novice neighbors a warm welcome. I hope the preceding counsel will aid your transition to life under the Big Sky. Obviously, volumes could be written on this subject. However, because the wind is currently dislodging the storm door from my house, I think it wise to end this piece. Who knows, dear newcomers, perhaps someday we shall meet and further discuss strategies for dealing with Montana's covert resource. Until then, happy sailing.

Bugged Buggy

A story worth the telling

Recently, I listened as two old friends of mine recounted an experience they had shared during their young adult years. As I listened to the uproarious account, it occurred to me that their narrative deserved a wider audience. So, with their encouragement, following is the story as told to me.

One day in May of 1975, Buck and his friend Moe (the names have been altered to protect the perpetrators) were inspecting some recently retired vehicles at Buck's ranch. To most folks, the 1960-era Dodge sedan would have looked like any of a thousand old cars languishing beside a barn. Yet, within that weathered hulk, the bright-eyed young men saw the makings of a first-class dune buggy.

Over the next month, in their spare time, the intrepid pair worked feverishly. The engine was fitted with a new battery, spark plugs and other needed accessories. Body parts were stripped from the chassis. A buggy frame and roll bars were installed. Finally, with Buck at the wheel, the daring duo went for a test drive down the Old Yellowstone Trail between Harrison and Willow Creek.

To this day, Buck swears he never saw that fresh cow pie lying on the road. Nonetheless, when ran over, its juicy contents surged upward through an opening in the recently altered floorboards. In less than a heartbeat, a stream of bovine manure was sprayed from Moe's belt buckle to the tip of his straw cowboy hat. Much to his credit, Buck restrained the guffaws racking his body well enough to bring the vehicle to a stop.

Despite his cohort's discomfort, Buck was mesmerized by the aesthetic properties of the trail mix stream. Bold and broad at the bottom, it tapered to a delicate pinnacle at the crown of Moe's hat. Further, the rich mahogany-brown droppings contrasted flawlessly with the light-tan of the straw Stetson. Then, a burst of obscenities startled Buck back to the moment.

Clearly, a major bug had been revealed in their buggy that cried out for modification. During the drive home, at his amigo's barked commands, Buck diligently avoided anything remotely resembling a cow patty. At the shop, Buck welded extra plating on the chassis floor while, in the nearby restroom, Moe gargled furiously. Nevertheless, youth does not abide despair for long. Soon, the buggy masters were cruising down the same road.

Shortly, Moe noticed an uncomfortable constriction. As luck would have it, the loose end of his old-style, waist-strap seat belt had dangled outside the frame, where it had been drawn around the front axle. Unaware of the crises next to him, Buck abruptly found himself being violently flailed about the head. Looking to his right, he saw the purple-faced, bug-eyed passenger frantically pointing at his mid-section. Buck quickly deduced that his amigo was in distress and stopped the buggy. Then, with Moe frantically motioning to the rear, he backed up. A loud sucking sound ensued.

Gamely, Buck suggested yet another design alteration. However, by then, Moe's mood had turned grim. He reckoned he was getting all the worst of it. So, with his sidekick holding his seat belt at arm's length, Buck drove dejectedly back to the ranch, where the ill-fated vehicle was parked beside the barn. Though their friendship survived, the two men never shared another trip in the bugged-buggy.

Ultimately, both men went on to successful business

careers. To this day, both agree the entrepreneurial spirit that inspired their future accomplishments, was blown to flame that spring day amidst the billowing dust and spewing compost of the Old Yellowstone Trail.

Small Town Tradition

Examining the rural Montana mindset

Right now as winter wanes and spring approaches, people are gathered to plan an annual tradition that has both entertained and amused me over the years. In tiny off-the-beaten-track villages amounting to little more than specks on the map, local dignitaries are hunkered down. For long hours, they toil to perpetuate a custom peculiar to sparsely populated areas like Southwest Montana.

On a given summer day, the fruits of their labors become evident. Then people who see each other on average three hundred days per year gather in the town's epicenter for the annual community parade. Reasons for such gala celebrations vary from patriotism, community pride, or simply the fact that the townsfolk neither starved nor froze to death through the winter. At the appointed time, one half the town lines the sidewalks (assuming there are any). Meanwhile the other half of the town's citizens cruise the main street mounted on assorted livestock, bicycles, motorized manure dispensers etc. and—they wave at one another.

Indeed, to the uninitiated, planning such a seemingly minor event might appear an easy task. However, it is important to keep in mind that the hamlets I am referring to can barely muster enough kids for a Class C school basketball team. Therefore, the logistics involved are complicated by the fact that often the main street is decidedly shorter than the length of the parade. With no place for surplus participants to gather, event organizers are left with little choice but to restrict the size of the review. Such circumstances can make for a cavalcade of very short duration indeed. In no time at all, the procession is over and everyone is left wondering what all the fuss was about.

In an effort to cope with this vexing problem, some of the finest minds in the state are hard at work trying to find a practical solution. Recently, when this very problem was discussed at a local watering hole, I heard a particularly engaging idea. In a bold break from tradition the question was posed: "Why not let the parade stand still and have the spectators march by?"

You could have heard a pin drop in the joint as envious minds silently pondered, "Why didn't I think of that?" The idea's genius lies in its simplicity. Utilizing the new standard, the parade could be left at its present length (approximately the span of the town).

At the same time, because matters would progress at the velocity of leisurely foot traffic, the procession would seem longer, thus killing two birds with one stone. Furthermore, the visionary brainstorm would provide the following additional benefits:

- Save fuel
- Make other small towns green with envy and—most importantly
- Allow additional time for folks to wave at one another.

If I dare say so myself, it is precisely this sort of out-of-the-box thinking that epitomizes the remarkably inventive mindset of rural Montanans. Only the coming of summer will tell if this exciting new concept is implemented.

Of course, any country boy knows you can't have a parade without a party afterwards to celebrate the parade. Who cares if the music is a trifle out of tune, the burgers are incinerated and a dog hoists his shank on the liquid refreshment cooler? In the spirit of the day, such trivialities are hardly worthy of note.

No doubt those from more metropolitan environs might be inclined to poke fun at such quaint local culture. However, to the denizens of diminutive towns such carrying on is perfectly reasonable. They understand the camaraderie that develops amongst people who live in isolated mountain nooks and prairie coulees, a long ways from nowhere. They also realize that the incessant flapping of digits is just an animated way of saying, “I know you. You’re one of us.”

Ultimately, it is up to those who enjoy such momentous occasions to acknowledge the hard work of the planners. Often, in the excitement of the pageant, those efforts are overlooked. I personally appreciate their labor very much. Living in a time of almost constant change, it is comforting to have customs that continue. As such, I hope this is one rite that never ends. For in truth, if the spectacles fade away, so will the towns. I would miss them both fearsome. So here’s to small town parades, may they march on in perpetuity. Oh yeah, and somebody keep an eye on that dog.

Entering the Developed World

Reflections on Harrison's recent technological invasion

Indisputably, it's the biggest event in Harrison since the celebrated laying of the sewer lines in the early 2000s. Three weeks ago, a small army of strange, helmeted men and their excavation machines showed up in town. Overnight, the community's population doubled. Local veterans opined that there hadn't been so much tracked machinery in such a small area since the Battle of the Bulge.

Then, in a disturbing turn of events, orange lines appeared on our streets. Popular consensus held that the cafe's daily liberal versus conservative political debate had finally gotten out of hand. Therefore, the lines had been painted by the police to mark the site of a fatal crime scene. As if that wasn't bad enough, the outsiders next began digging holes all over town. For a while, it looked as though our quiet village had suffered an invasion of body snatchers.

Fortunately, those dramatic scenarios were put to rest when locals noticed the invaders' pickup trucks bore the logo of a regional telephone service provider. Soon after, to everyone's relief, word got out that the strangers were here to lay fiber-optic cables for their company's Harrison customers.

In no time at all, streets and alleys were being excavated in mass. To everyone's amazement, at various pinch points, Harrison actually experienced traffic congestion. In one instance, four cars were stopped for almost a minute. A riot nearly broke out. To avoid further hostilities, some citizens used all-terrain vehicles to straddle the railroad tracks behind the town and bypass the pinch points altogether.

Things got even more exciting when the cable crews began to lay lines through people's lawns. Because the workers were entering private property, misgivings were heightened. As a result, local gardeners could be seen grimly guarding their treasured plots with brandished shovels. For a while, the tension was tangible. Nonetheless, in the end, all the primary cables were installed without horticultural mishap. The final hookups are to take place sometime later.

Certainly, I am no electronic communications expert. However, from what I have gathered, a Harrison customer's home phone, Internet, and TV service will all be contained in one fiber-optic cable. Additionally, because said cable will be buried underground, TV clients may no longer have to sweep snow from a satellite dish. Most impressively, the fiber-optic cable will provide a lot more bandwidth than does the current copper wire hookups. Hence, data-transfer speeds will increase greatly. All of which means, when the town's customers are on the Internet, their computers will run much faster.

Conversely, I wonder if human eyes, like those of a dog with its head hung out the window of a speeding car, will be harmed by extended viewing of the blizzard of flashing images? Similarly, what about the potentially disastrous adverse effects of mega-speed Internet surfing during an earthquake? Only time will tell if my concerns are legitimate.

Ultimately, when the fiber optics installation is completed, Harrison will have officially entered the developed world, and—I'm not sure we're ready. Furthermore, I'm not sure the developed world is ready for that momentous transition either. Nevertheless, like folks in many other small Montana towns, our citizens are remarkably adaptable. Given time, there's little doubt we will adjust to this newest technological invasion. Then maybe everyone can put their shovels away.

Bear Trap Canyon Grand Prix

Recalling the harrowing experience of surviving a vehicular hurricane

If last year is any indication, about 11 million nonresidents will visit our state this year. One day last week, while driving round trip from Harrison to Bozeman, I believe I encountered every one of those visitors. To say the traffic was worrisome would be akin to calling a grizzly bear a panda.

Initially, I drove north from Harrison to Three Forks. The first thing I noticed was the extraordinary number of vehicles on the road. Even on that two-lane highway, the 70-mph speed limit was not fast enough for them. I watched incredulously as cars zoomed past me on blind corners.

Eventually, I got stuck behind a pickup truck, pulling a large camper at 55 mph. In no time, motorists were backed up for a long distance. Because the oncoming traffic was also heavy, no one who valued life dared pass. Nonetheless, I knew it was just a matter of time until a fearless (brainless) thrill-seeker would throw caution to the wind. As the seconds ticked by, the tension became unbearable.

Then, the fourth car back pulled out to pass. As he roared by, the driver's facial expression mimicked that of one those wackos that dive off towering cliffs in a flying squirrel suit. I watched aghast as approaching cars began edging toward the side of the road. At the last instant, the NASCAR wannabe swerved so sharply in front of the camper-pulling pickup that he nearly scraped its front bumper off. The pickup's driver then wisely pulled over to let the congestion go by and, I suspect, examine his Fruit of the Looms.

Near Three Forks, I entered the freeway and headed for Bozeman. The traffic was beyond awful. Again, traveling at the 75-mph speed limit was considered dawdling. It felt as though I had been sucked into an overpowering vehicular hurricane and was being swept to certain disaster.

Sure enough, a motor home soon began to pass me. Apparently, the lumbering vehicle's operator, who obviously hadn't driven anything larger than a Mini Cooper coupe before, lost sight of me in his rear-view mirror. So, he began edging the humongous, rolling residence into my lane—while it was still directly alongside my car! In yet another bowel-stirring scenario, I was forced to abandon the freeway, and screech to a stop on the side of the road.

Finally, I arrived at Wal-Mart in Bozeman. Having reached the eye of the storm, I was about to get a break from the hectic traffic, or so I thought. To my immeasurable irritation, the scourge of shoppers operated their shopping carts just like they drove their cars. Once, when a grossly overloaded cart was rammed past mine, I was pasted up against the side of the frozen-food aisle freezers. Though I can't prove it, I'm pretty sure the culprit was the driver of the aforementioned motor home.

Hoping to encounter less traffic on the way home, I took State Route 84 to Norris. Before long, I became a wholly unwilling participant in an impromptu Beartrap Canyon Grand Prix. Yet again, I was caught up in an automotive tempest and fairly propelled through the Canyon's hairpin curves at maniacal speeds. Miraculously, I arrived in Norris in one piece.

Finally, as Harrison came into view, I felt grateful for being delivered from the vehicular hurricane. Additionally, I suddenly saw the wisdom of paying to have a drone deliver groceries to my door. At any rate, I may not leave the cloistered confines of Harrison again until winter.

Dumpster Drama

Recalling some memorable trash exploits

Recently, I spent time reminiscing about the many, storied misadventures involving Harrison and Pony residents. While pondering past times, it soon became apparent that many of those hallowed events had occurred at an under-appreciated location: the local dumpster.

As a case in point, one day a few winters ago, I watched as a pickup truck, pulling a garbage trailer with high plywood walls, backed up the dumpster's snow-covered ramp. The driver came to a stop with the trailer just inches from the waste container's edge, and the truck positioned on the slope. Soon, trash bags and other unsavory items virtually flew from the back of the trailer.

Suddenly, a shout of alarm rang out. The old boy's zeal for his work had shaken the trailer so vigorously as to cause the truck tires to lose grip with the ramp's icy surface. Consequently, the pickup and trailer, with its hapless occupant still on board, were streaking downward toward some bushes at the bottom of the ramp.

In shocked amusement, I witnessed a splendid athletic feat unfold before my very eyes. With feet spread wide, knees bent deeply and upper extremities flailing frantically, the valiant rubbish slinger desperately tried to maintain balance. He did a swell job too, right up until the truck hit those bushes, whereupon, the victim suffered a very non-athletic face-plant against the trailer's front wall.

As foul words coursed the air, I struggled mightily to stifle unfitting snickers and chortles. Of course, upon recovering my composure, I fairly dashed to offer aid. Fortunately, other than a barked nose, the disheveled victim was fine. Finally, it occurred to the old boy that it might be advantageous to put chains on the truck tires. After so doing, the remaining garbage was gingerly expelled without further theatrics.

Another dumpster drama occurred during the summer months. It seems that, while throwing trash from his pickup's tailgate, a friend of mine lost his balance and fell, head-first, into the container. Luckily, said waste depository was partially full at the time, and he landed on semi-soft garbage bags. Nevertheless, there was some bitterness regarding the stale french fry that, on impact, lodged in one of his nostrils. Though unintentional, there's no denying that my amigo's performance elevated dumpster diving to a purer form.

To that point in time, the only positive aspect concerning said incident was that no one had witnessed the embarrassing exhibition. Hoping to avoid further humiliation, my pal hurriedly stacked garbage bags against a corner of the dumpster. After climbing the stack, he managed to grasp the metal container's top edge and began to pull himself up. Naturally, as is the way of life, before the poor wretch could extract himself, two vehicles arrived on the scene. Word of his mortifying misfortune spread like a sonic boom.

Finally, I recently observed two teenage girls flinging garbage bags into the local dumpster. They used a spinning motion like that of a discuss-thrower. The young ladies' exaggerated ballerina-like trash bag release was a thing of beauty. Not only that, their aim was unerring. Soon, it struck me that what I was seeing was the next generation of dumpster drama contestants, honing their skills. Smiling inwardly, I drove home knowing the torch had been passed.

Bona Fide Bitter Cold

Survival tips for an old-time Montana winter

During a recent cold spell, I recall watching the weather report on a local television station. The forecaster stood beside a southwest Montana map, on which appeared the following warning: "Bitter Cold Tonight: 10 Degrees Below Zero." With visions of long ago winters flashing in my mind, I couldn't help but notice how the definition of "bitter cold" has changed over the years.

No doubt, everyone has a lowest, low-temperature story to tell. For me, that memorable moment occurred during a New Year's Eve dance at the Norris Bar about forty years ago. The joint was jammed. The night was so glacial that every one of the approximately seventy-five cars outside was left running. At the stroke of midnight, with a crowd of revelers assembled behind me, I scraped the ice from a window through which the outside thermometer could be seen. When I announced the recorded temperature as "45-degrees-below-zero," a raucous cheer erupted. Three weeks later, the mercury finally crept above zero. Now that's bona fide bitter cold.

Thanks to old-time Montana winters, I learned a few things about surviving such conditions. Most crucially, I discovered that, during daylight hours, thermometers often register deceptively high readings. For this reason, I developed some practical methods for ensuring that conditions are humanly endurable before one blithely dashes outside. They are as follows:

- Check that the exterior cold doesn't penetrate the entrance door by more than two feet.

- Look outside for dogs peeing next to steaming clothes dryer vents.
- Scan the neighborhood for frozen, white-blackbirds hanging upside down from power lines.
- Watch out for jumper cables being blown across the hard snow with gloves still frozen to the handles.
- Look for suspiciously stiff cats with their extended paws piteously embedded into front doors.
- Notice any stationary, purple-lipped people shivering uncontrollably beside their newspaper boxes.
- Call your next-door neighbor and tell him his chimney is on fire. When he emerges from his house, notice how far he makes it before suffering loss of motor skills, delirium or other symptoms of severe hypothermia.
- Set a cup of hot coffee just inside the storm door. Then watch to see if it freezes solid while steam still wafts from the lid.
- Toss a piece of bread out of the front door, and then observe the pecking birds for signs of beakbite (frostbite of the beak).
- Open the front door and thrust your index finger outside for ten seconds to test for temperature and wind-chill factor. Then, examine said finger for discoloration and numbness.
- Lastly, if said index finger proves to be frostbitten, stick it down your throat and while still coughing and hacking, call in sick for work.

In the end, here's hoping that old-time Montana winters are a thing of the past. If not, I trust that other bona fide, bitter cold survivors will follow my selfless model and share their frozen appendage-learned lessons with the uninitiated. In the meantime, remember, "never trust a thermometer."

Kindly Gestures

Some reflexions on an ill-considered walk

During my time in Montana, I have observed that there are only a limited number of nice days in an average year. So, when a tolerable one occurs, no matter what month it falls in, I go outside and enjoy it. After all, it may be a long time before another such day comes along. Consequently, when the temperature recently rose to the high 40's, I was raring to go for a walk. Because all the local dirt roads were covered with ice, I decided to walk alongside US 287 on the Sand Creek Hill, north of Harrison. I drove about a third of the way down the hill's steepest section, parked my car, bounced out, and struck a trot for the summit.

At first, I was cold. Lucky for me, my physical fitness level proved to be a tad shy of what I had anticipated. Therefore, my body temperature climbed to a point where my clothing began to emit steam. My trot transitioned into a trudge, and my exhalations became robust enough to rattle a mile marker sign. By the time I reached the halfway point of the ascent, I felt as though I was climbing Hollowtop Mountain in my fishing waders.

Then, a motorist approached from behind and stopped. Convinced that my car had conked out, she offered me a ride. When I responded—"No thanks, I'm just walking,"—the kindly woman's jaw plunged in shocked disbelief. I'm pretty sure she thought she'd encountered a deranged practitioner of extreme sports for the elderly.

Periodically, to ward off pre-rigor mortis (arthritic stiffening), I stopped and did some stretching exercises.

Apparently, the accompanying contortions convinced several motorists that I was in the throes of a life-threatening cardiac malfunction. They were so concerned that I worried someone might exit their vehicle, slam me to the ground and zap me with a heart defibrillator. Next, a fully-loaded tractor trailer stopped. To my amazement, the driver even backed his truck up to see if I was okay. Humbled, I watched the sainted soul shift through every gear while regaining speed up the hill.

During the one-half hour it took me to reach the summit, nine vehicles stopped to offer a ride. Some were strangers, some were folks I knew. My walk turned out to be a roundabout way to meet new people and visit with neighbors.

As I thought about it, I began to feel bad about being the cause of so many kindly gestures. I had to grant that, if I had driven up to a golden-ager steaming up a steep hill in the middle of February, I too would have been concerned. I also would have concluded that his vehicle had broken down, and if someone didn't give him a lift, the old boy would be found frozen stiff beside the road come morning. At that, I had to admit that I too would have stopped.

Ultimately, as I see it, there are two lessons to be learned from my ill-considered decision to walk that day: 1.) Don't be misled by the calloused hostility so often portrayed in current news reports and 2.) In the end, the good guys are going to win. To those who recognize themselves in this article, "Thank you." You are the reason I choose to live here.

Sitting on the Bench

A lesson learned through observation

For many years, I observed old people sitting on benches, feeding the pigeons. Never did it occur to me that, one day, I would join their ranks. Nonetheless, last spring, I began to sit, periodically, on a sidewalk bench on the main street of Harrison. I did so to relax while watching the sun set. Regrettably, the town's few, unrefined pigeons weren't savvy enough to know that bench sitters are supposed to feed them.

Sure enough, as in any small town, such a major happening did not go unnoticed for long. Because of my customary appearance on the bench, I was quickly anointed as Harrison's own Kaw Liga the Wooden Indian. Hence, I decided it would be prudent to wave at the passing drivers to avoid the possibility of pedestrians trying to snuff their cigarettes out on my forehead. Lamentably, before long I developed carpal tunnel nerve restrictions in both wrists. So, I began nodding my head in the direction of passing motorists instead. Unsurprisingly, that adjustment resulted in my being likened to a life-size, bobble-head toy. Despite such indignities, I stayed the course.

To their credit, unlike the pigeons, the village's dogs stopped by, fully expecting to be fed. Observing law-abiding citizens executing convenient, but unlawful, U-turns when driving away from the Post Office, was always entertaining. Once, the local school's cross-country team trotted past me on their way out of town.

Like any concerned older (wiser) citizen would, I warned them that, if they insisted on running around as they were, they were going to get tired. Surprisingly, everyone agreed but the coach.

However, the most upsetting observation I made concerned the amount of traffic that journeyed through our isolated outpost on any given day. When one considers that from my centrally-located bench I could see both the northern and southern boundaries of Harrison, the number of drivers seemed excessive. After all, it's not like the town is a suburb of a mega-metropolis.

Then again, it is also a fact that Harrison is located on US 287, a major interstate travel route. With that in mind, I found it harder to fault travelers for where our founding fathers situated the town. Still, the traffic was always "there," which made it difficult for me to relax.

Especially anti-relaxing were the tractor-trailer operators who applied their Jake-brakes in order to slow down when entering the town. Suffice it to say, many a glorious sunset was dimmed by the sudden eruption of their thunderous, flatulence-like rumblings. Likewise, car drivers who graciously rolled down their windows, so I too could savor their raucous rap, overwhelmed any semblance of tranquility.

During April, I decided to conduct an experiment. From my perch on the bench, whenever the visible north and south portions of the road were empty of motorists, I tried counting thirty seconds to see if they would remain so during that span. Sad to say, after numerous attempts, it never happened. Within that one-half minute period, invariably, vehicles could be seen approaching from one or both directions.

At that point, I decided to stop swimming against the inevitable current. Instead of complaining about the traffic, I began to wish the individual drivers well. Subsequently, I began to envision them as people, not vehicles. Strangely enough, more and more folks began waving at me. Who knows, with so many people witnessing me sitting on the bench, the Harrison bobble-head toy might soon be the subject of a country-western song.

Regional Repossession

Observing an annual Tri-city tradition

Well, autumn has officially arrived in the Tri-city region. The great throngs of summer tourists have returned home. As always, their departure has led to a temporary sense of emptiness. At the same time, a suppressed pique over the vacationers' summer-long occupation of our treasured native sod has begun to reveal itself. In fact, if one watches closely, the subtle signs of regional repossession are already evident.

For instance, nowadays, many Tri-city citizens refuse to wait in line at the local gas station. Instead, they insist on circling around the station for however long it takes for a pump to open. Then, after filling up, the assertive residents make it a point to check the engine oil and air pressure in the spare tire. Finally, in a blatant display of jurisdiction, they intentionally leave their cars sitting at the pump while going inside to scrutinize the snack rack.

At our regional eateries, deposed, disgruntled resident coffee slurpers are, with great fanfare, re-commandeering their privileged stools at the counters where "personal" mugs await them. Additionally, tourists ordering Americano, espresso, and flavored lattes are being supplanted by locals ordering starter fluid, forty-weight, or morning mud. People whistle loudly while loitering in the restrooms.

As well, traffic has decreased dramatically on the Pony road and on the stretch of highway between Harrison and Norris. Consequently, motor homes are being displaced by grain trucks, and four-wheel-drive pickups are reclaiming their status as the "monarchs" of those roads. Madison County license plates now outnumber out-of-state plates. Perhaps most heartening, parking spaces are now available in front of our community taverns. Inside the joints, locally-revered, country-western music is drowning out the last remnants of summer's hip hop, and rap recordings, on the juke boxes.

At the grocery store, lengthy lines of six or more customers are being replaced by individual patrons, who carefully examine the newspaper on the counter while the checkout person finishes a game of solitaire on a smart phone. Next, they pay with cash, orally counting out each coin. In the seats of vehicles parked outside, hardworking cow dogs are taking the place of pampered poodles.

Also, traffic on the road to Harrison Lake is a fraction of what it was. So, resident drivers are currently bold enough to glance off the road and savor the desolate landscape. Occasionally, the brazen yokels even lower the windows and point at things. With the disappearance of speed boats and jet skies at the lake, local fishermen are blissfully recapturing their beloved turf.

At the post offices, patrons are inserting their letters into the "out of town" slot—one at a time. Subsequently, they casually sort through the new mail. Lastly, in an epic act of tenure, many perform the notorious (illegal) Tri-city u-turn on the highway in front of the buildings.

On the land bordering our unpaved country lanes, now that the tourist-traffic-induced dust clouds have settled, native deer are reclaiming their grazing rights. Two pickups, parked side by side, in the middle of said lanes (while the drivers flop their gums), is becoming a common sight again. In the barrow pits, the number of discarded fruit smoothie containers is being overtaken by the number of discarded snus cans.

In the end, observing the many small, yet, earnest acts of regional repossession has lifted my spirits considerably. After all, along with the arrival of autumn, they signal a return to Tri-city normalcy.

Thank goodness for annual traditions.

Swede's Gate

Recalling the work of a local legend

Imagine if you will a pristine October morning with fresh tracking snow on the ground. Three men in a pickup truck bounce along a primitive road, miles from the nearest town. Soon, they approach a barbed wire fence. Heartbeats surge when about 1,000 yards beyond the fence, twenty-five elk appear on the horizon. Horns glean in the early light. Suddenly, the truck surges ahead. All those lucky hunters need do is get through that fence and they'll have those wapiti deadly mortal in their gun sights.

The truck screeches to a stop before a gate. The man on the passenger side jumps out to open it. With trigger fingers twitching, the other hunters watch as, with eyeballs squinted shut and ears laid back, the hapless hunter compresses the gate with all his might—to no avail. Pointing frantically at the elk, the two men join their companion who complains of having swallowed his Copenhagen snus. Soon all three men are grunting, purple-faced, in a desperate effort to pry open the accursed portal. The scuffed ground, heel furrows, and overturned rocks testify to a colossal struggle but in the end, the gate remains unconquered and unopened. Muttering expletives, the hunters watch helplessly as the elk scamper out of sight unscathed. At last, one hunter exclaims, "Congratulations fellers, we've just encountered a true work of Madison County art: a dreaded 'Swede's gate.'"

Swede is a retired cowboy of no small renown in the Harrison-Pony-Norris area. In his younger days, he was a man of unusual physical strength. Having been raised in this locale, Swede was well aware of the power of wind to shape his world. Even in this region notorious for its howling winds, the Norris wind stands apart. It has been known to reduce strong men to raging lunatics and stones to powder. Subject to its ravages, any slipshod fencing effort would be rendered a swaying, sagging eyesore in short order. Add to that the weight of snowdrifts and it becomes apparent that gates in this vicinity need to be constructed, above all else, to be durable.

With those facts in mind, Swede built his gates to stand the test of time. Posts were anchored deep and wires stretched as taut as his prodigious strength would allow. When finished, they fairly sang with rigid perfection. So great was his commitment to craftsmanship that there is little doubt when the frozen finger of the next ice age nudges up against one of his gates, Swede would fully expect it to still be "tolerable tight."

Regrettably, Swede never appreciated the magnitude of his own strength. He just didn't understand that gates he could easily open often caused others hernias. Moreover, those few man enough to wrestle open one of Swede's gates were condemned to speak with a decidedly soprano lilt for a week or so afterward.

In an effort to avoid such humiliating impairment, some of our shrewder citizens proposed the idea of carrying violin bows in their hunting rigs. Then, when encountering a suspiciously stiff-looking gate, the bow is laid across the top wire. If then, they are able to perform a passable rendition of Beethoven's Violin Concerto, the hunters are forewarned of dealing with Swede's handiwork, and can seek more accommodating access.

Now in his eighties, Swede sits home every hunting season, content in knowing that folks are still gathering at isolated gates to celebrate his work and praise his name. Although his gates are a subject of some contention, I know of no one in this area that doesn't admire the man. He has become one of our revered local elders and with good reason. For many, Swede epitomizes the ruggedly independent people that settled this land, who by their example set the founding principals of this great state so sturdily that they were certain to stand the test of time. Here's to you Swede, may it ever be so.

Highest Low Temperature

Some observations concerning a cherished Harrison tradition

Every winter, it's an ongoing happening. Though it's an unofficial sort of thing, there's no denying it's real. Just beneath the surface of feigned cordiality, the competition is fierce. Even the wording of its coveted award can be confusing. Nonetheless, when the snow has settled, winners smugly reign while losers enviously sulk.

After each winter storm, every adult in Harrison capable of movement scrambles from bed well before daylight. Instinctively, they grab the flashlight left purposefully lying on the cabinet close by their beds. Without delay, they walk to those windows in their homes that face a thermometer.

Shortly, in what sounds like a scourge of beavers feverishly gnawing in the forests, ice is being scraped from windows across the length and breadth of the town. Next, like the rudely awakened eyes of fire-spewing dragons, beams of light pierce the darkness all around. Then, with their flashlights clearly focused on their thermometers, the beady-eyed residents wait for the mercury to inch downward to its lowest point. Somewhat confusingly, that lowest point (also represented by the largest-negative-number) is referred to locally as the "highest-low-temperature."

No one in Harrison knows for sure how the "largest negative number" came to be interpreted as the "highest low temperature" and—no one cares. All that matters is that the latter term has become the accepted norm. So, with their cherished figures in hand, the citizens migrate downtown where feigned cordial greetings are exchanged. Then, the undeclared competition begins when someone poses the incendiary question that every ear has been straining to hear: "How cold was it at your place this morning?"

Immediately, the verbal mittens come off and folks begin barking out their individual temperature recordings. In a scene reminiscent of a fast-paced auction, each submitted temperature observation is quickly trumped by an even more bone marrow-solidifying counter observation. Soon, the noise level rises to a crescendo rivaling that of the New York Stock Exchange during a market rally. Finally, after all the recordings have been compared, the unofficial "highest-low-temperature in Harrison" winner is announced. Within seconds, aside from muffled grumbling, quiet is restored.

Considering all the fuss, one would think the reward for such a chilling honor would be something along the lines of a frozen turkey. Instead, because the event is only quasi-formal, the winner is awarded something far more valuable: community bragging rights. Until the next winter storm blows in, the chosen one savors a temporary level of elevated community status. Meanwhile, the rest of the townsfolk have to endure his or her intolerable snobbery with barely concealed resentment.

Alas, one local rogue was recently rumored to have used a portable fan to blow icy wind against his thermometer. That would have increased the wind-chill factor thereby lowering his highest-low-temperature reading. Clearly, such skullduggery cannot go unchallenged.

Consequently, there has been talk of forming a "verification vigilance committee," whose job it would be to authenticate every temperature submission. As a result, the only acceptable readings would be those recorded on a cell phone selfie photo. Said picture would need to display the date, the time, the submitter's face and unencumbered hand along with the thermometer reading in the background (aka a thermometer photo bomb).

Ultimately, the problem is that enacting the above measures may threaten the event's unofficial status which would only confuse matters even more. Only time will tell if Harrison's cherished winter custom will endure. We'll keep ya posted.

Amusing Arctic Anecdotes

Some Not-So-Scary, Snow-Plowing Stories of Yore

In the late 1960s, I drove snowplows on the State Highway Department's Harrison section. Unsurprisingly, during that time I experienced my share of hair-raising moments. Conversely, I also recall some amusing events. For instance, there was the morning I was plowing east of Norris, on State Route 84, where the road closely paralleled the Madison River. The road's surface was a sheet of ice. A dense fog severely limited visibility.

Suddenly, a deer popped into view just yards ahead. The flustered critter tried to leave the road, but fell on the ice. At that point, I had two choices: 1) try to avoid it and likely slide into the river or 2) hit the deer. Expecting an unfortunate outcome, I watched as the doe vanished beneath the plow.

Directly, amidst the plow-thrown stream of snow and ice, I spied the old girl sailing over the roadside fence. The wretched creature soon thumped to the ground in a billowing cloud of snow. To my disbelief, the rumpled animal then bounced up, shook herself off and trotted away. Driving on, I wondered if that deer knew how lucky she was. After all, not many creatures are privileged to start their day in such an uplifting manner.

Another amusing event occurred during an early snowstorm that struck on a Labor Day weekend. Approaching the Norris Hill from the north, I noticed a car parked beside the road. The occupants were an elderly couple from the deep South who were vacationing in Montana for the first time. The naive tourists were convinced they were about to enter a form of arctic cyclone and be buried alive in a glacier alongside the remains of woolly mammoths. Only after a lengthy series of deep breathing exercises, did they agree to let me drive them to McAllister in their car.

On the way, the old gentleman asked if it always snowed in Montana during the first week of September. I replied that it wasn't uncommon. Aghast, his wife then asked what time of the year it stopped snowing. When I replied, "early May," my fair-weather acquaintances succumbed to inconsolable homesickness. All my attempts to describe the splendors of a Montana summer fell on deaf ears. When we finally arrived in McAllister, the disenchanted tourists sped south without a backward glance.

Beyond doubt, the most memorable event occurred one night on the Norris Hill during a late winter storm. Snow was falling heavily, and (surprise-surprise) the wind was howling. Unable to keep the road open, I called headquarters to notify the radio stations that the Norris Hill was closed to traffic.

Later, I came eyeball-bulgingly close to hitting a car buried in a snow drift beside the road. Convinced that a distressed citizen had gotten stuck in a perilous position, I fairly dashed to the rescue. When asked if he knew the road was closed, the driver replied, "Yup, but I get better radio reception for the district basketball tournament from up here than I can get in town." After I promised to place a bouquet of long stemmed skunk cabbages at the spot where his car had been bashed over the hillside by another vehicle, he reconsidered and went home.

Ultimately, I accumulated many amusing arctic anecdotes during my snow plowing days. Despite the hair-raising accounts, it is those not-so-scary stories of yore that remain foremost in my memory.

Balanced Perspectives

Factors to consider during the annual surge of visitors

Warm weather has arrived, and the Tri-cities area will soon be teeming with out-of-state vacationers. Obviously, this isn't the preferred time of the year for residents who consider the region to be grossly overpopulated. At the same time, it's helpful to bear in mind that many summer vacationers envision our locality as a sparsely settled boondocks. Such divergent conceptions can lead to misunderstandings. Hence, in an effort to advance resident-visitor camaraderie, I feel compelled to offer the following balanced perspectives.

To begin, someone needs to inform portly male tourists with sparrow legs, they just don't look good in flaming red shorts. At the same time, it's only fair to concede that tourists have valid cause to stare at the distended lower lips of local Copenhagen snuff chewers. Furthermore, there's no call for excessive chewer indignation when asked if said abnormality is a genetic mutation. After all, it may be a legitimate expression of concern.

Admittedly, Harrison's residents do get spoiled during the slow-paced winter months. Consequently, summer visitors should strive to understand the anguish townsfolk suffer when forced to stand in a line of more than two people at the town's grocery store. Then again, townsfolk should consider that, for many travelers, having to shave twice while waiting to check out of an urban Wal-Mart is normal. As well, there's the annual strife that arises when a local customer stops at the town's cafe and discovers an outsider occupying his seat. At such traumatic moments, it's crucial to grasp that the nonresident offender is blissfully unaware of his or her appalling breach of village etiquette. On the other hand, when attempting to strike up a conversation with the ousted resident, the outsider needs to realize that the question, "What's new in Harrison?" isn't likely to spark protracted discussion.

Once again, Pony drivers will need to be alert for tourists, strolling four-abreast, up the Pony Road, firmly convinced it's a paved cow path. Still, when exposed to sweeping scenery, it is quite normal for habitually cramped city dwellers to exhibit curious behavior. Additionally, Pony hikers need to be sympathetic when encountering blue-faced flatlanders who thought that 8,543-foot elevation, Hollowtop Lake was a good place to practice their backstroke.

No doubt the citizens of Norris will be most radically impacted. The sad truth is there will be summer days when the number of travelers parked at the town's gas station exceeds the metropolitan population. But then, with all those extra people around, the town's mosquitoes can choose from a larger pool of victims. Furthermore, sharing sob stories with travelers about the price of gas may provide a compensating level of interstate bonding.

Moreover, area drivers best be on guard when approaching those dips in the road that can't be seen until one is upon them. All too often, an out-of-state car may be found stopped in the middle of the traffic lane. Upon screeching to an exhilarating stop, the dismayed locals may discover the starry-eyed occupants ogling (what is to them) an exotic buck antelope. After peeling their lips from the windshield, the affected resident motorists should demonstrate our legendary cordiality by not foaming at the mouth while registering their displeasure.

In sum, here's hoping the above balanced perspectives promote a mutual spirit of open-mindedness during the annual surge of visitors. With luck, visitors will experience our culture (such as it is), and Tri-city residents will receive desperately needed news from the outside world. That sounds fair to me.

Chlorophyll Challenged

Confessions of a non-flower person

Not long ago, while getting my mail at the Harrison Post Office, I overheard a conversation between some local folks. Not surprisingly, with spring fast approaching, the discussion concerned tending flowers. As I listened, I couldn't help but admire their extensive knowledge of how to make things grow. When invited to join the discussion, I sheepishly confessed, "the only thing I've ever grown is fungus on a loaf of bread."

Pathetic as that may seem for a citizen of an agricultural town, there was good reason for my seemingly appalling shortcoming. To explain, for many years, I rented my dwellings. Hence, the landlords took care of such tedious trivialities as lawns and posies. By so craftily doing, I was able to invest my free time in more gratifying pursuits such as fishing, camping and hiking. However, as often happens, recent events have drastically changed my lifestyle.

To begin, not long ago, I purchased my present home, around which the previous owner had planted numerous flowers. Not knowing what to do, when growing season arrived, I let things take their natural course. Soon, the sown beds were sprouting a fetching blend of emaciated flowers and vibrant noxious weeds. Urged on by the steely stares of neighbors, I grudgingly submitted to trying my hand at tending the barely blossoming finery.

While pulling weeds, for the first time ever, I failed to notice that, in their early stages of development, many buds look remarkably like grass. Consequently, at least as many plants were uprooted as were weeds and grass. Furthermore, it took a while for me to grasp that, when pulling weeds, it is best to position the feet outside the pansy bed. Thus, I proved to be the antithesis of the romantic saying, "flowers bloom where you have trod." More realistically, it could be said, "flowers wither where Art has stomped."

Building on that stellar start, I proceeded to irrigate. Before long, it became apparent that tulip beds don't require the same volume of water as do rice paddies. Despite my finest efforts, a number of plants somehow withstood the ravages of my care-taking and bloomed. However, it wasn't long before it was evident that I had more than just lack of experience to overcome.

Some folks are born with a "green thumb." Not me. I was born with "photosynthesis-purging paws." Compared to my chlorophyll-choking caress, Tordon is perfumed bubble bath. In my jinxed hands, even Miracle Grow acts as a defoliant similar to Agent Orange. For instance, the petals on my rose bushes aren't nearly as impressive as the lethal, fang-like thorns. They don't just tear clothing, they crave blood. Spiders fear to tread the hollyhocks by the shed. Once, I'm pretty sure I observed one of those blossoms that open and follow the sun's arc across the sky, abruptly reverse direction at my approach.

Conversely, that which I intentionally try to kill, flourishes. When spraying for dandelions, everything dies but the dandelions. After being doused to saturation, leafy spurge rebounds to the dimensions of a Costa Rican rain forest. In desperation, I even considered napalm. However, the cost in neighborly relations proved prohibitive.

In the final analysis, there's no denying that, to flowers, I am the personification of a biblical plaque. As things stand now, I am considering plastic flowers and Astroturf. Hopefully, I can't kill them. If so, I'll have no choice but to unpack the fishing pole, hiking shoes and tent. Being chlorophyll-challenged is a heavy burden, but—it is what it is.

Spontaneous Salutations

Thoughts on restoring an old tradition

Many years ago in this area, it was customary to extend a goodwill greeting when entering a household. I refer to such time-honored salutations as: "Hello this house," "Good health to this house," and "Greetings to all." By so doing, guests expressed both respect and concern for their neighbors. Regrettably, over time, that quaint custom has fallen from practice. As a result, our hallmark reputation for neighborliness has been tarnished. Such an insufferable thought obliged me to attempt restoration of that long-forgotten rite of civility. It occurred to me that, by including our numerous small-town cafes on my "spontaneous salutations" list, more people will be touched by each heartfelt oration. Thus, the full recovery of our storied image could be hastened.

In yet another burst of awareness, the thought occurred that the majority of locals prefer to sink their chili chompers into the lip-smacking, taste-bud-flipping, stomach-stuffing meals that are the norm in these parts. Thus, the first step of my plan had to consist of composing proclamations to suit those eating preferences.

Lastly, as with any finely choreographed production, accompanying animated gestures of sincerity (flourishing removal of headwear, sweeping arm motions etc.) also had to be perfected. With all the particulars duly identified, I set to work. Following is my initial list of uplifting gastronomical good wishes:

- "May your coffee trigger invigorating pupil constriction/dilation and spark the first detectable heartbeat of the day."

- "May your sticky buns be sufficiently gooey to challenge your Polygrip."
- "May your eggs be a textural balance of runny and rubbery, your hash browns brittle, and your sourdough toast pungent."
- "May your pancakes be light as Styrofoam, and your maple syrup flow like 10-30 weight, motor oil."
- "May your biscuits be densely fibrous, your peppery gravy cause profuse perspiration, and your sausage be odiferous."
- "May your omelets be outsized, swathed with cheese, and heaped with fiery peppers."
- "May your mashed potatoes be lumpy, your gravy shovel worthy, and your chicken-fried steak chewy enough to require on-site flossing."
- "May your waitress remain courteous while spilling scalding coffee in your lap."

As can be seen, the potential benevolent greetings are as numerous as the array of foods served. Clearly, the moment is a hand. However, at the same time, it is important to keep in mind that folks require time to readjust to old traditions. As such, I can readily envision my early efforts being misinterpreted as the ravings of one who forgot to take his meds. In the worse scene scenario, even brusque eviction from the premises is possible. Surely a lesser man would be embarrassed, but not me. Fortunately, having previously endured unwarranted indignities for various other reasons has thickened my sensibilities.

Consequently, I embark on my noble endeavor with patience and steadfast determination, optimistic that our neighborly rite of yore will, once again, be embraced. Who knows, our remote corner of Montana might spawn a nationwide trend of goodwill spontaneous salutations. I'll keep ya posted.

A Joyous Clamor

Rediscovering a familiar melody in the midst of a tempest

The racket was loud enough to wake the dead. If it had been the consequence of an out-of-control party, I would have called the police. However, as I drove closer, the sounds became more distinct. Shortly, it became plain that the foul perpetrators were waterfowl.

Every spring, for many years, I have made it a practice to drive out to Harrison Lake (aka Willow Creek Reservoir) to greet the returning migratory birds. This year, by late March, the lake was free of ice. Consequently, it was a magnet for feathered travelers.

Obviously, the birds were communicating. However, they all seemed to be shouting the same thing—at the same time. Like a bunch of giddy third-graders on the first day of school, their communal exuberance was palpable. Still, in the midst of all that clamor, I detected a familiar melody.

Luckily, by Harrison Lake standards, the wind was still relatively mild (i. e. it wasn't bouncing frogs off my windshield). Except for the birds, I had the lake to myself. Presently, I set up my spotting scope and began to examine the visitors.

First to catch my eye were the tundra swans. All white, except for their black bills and legs, they stood in sharp contrast to the overcast day. Their large wings flopped wildly as they shuffled across the water in nearly continual motion. Not far away, the Canadian geese were engaged in similar bedlam. Ducks would land, then take off and fly around the lake again. After scrutinizing the water, I decided to scope the surrounding prairie.

As of yet, the east side of Harrison Lake is undeveloped.

Therefore, what greets the eye is a grand expanse of nothing and, at the same time, everything. After a while, I located approximately one hundred elk on the prairie off toward Red Mountain. Viewed at 45-power, they looked to be in good shape. Then, a car load of fisherman showed up. From past experience, I knew that was a bad omen.

Sure enough, no sooner had the unsuspecting anglers set up their chairs, coolers and fishing rods, than a sound like that of a run-away freight train came barreling up Norwegian Creek from the south. Immediately, I recognized it as one of Harrison Lake's dreaded "spontaneous, concrete-outhouse-fracturing, bluster-gusters."

Before the fishermen could reach their car, the raging wind struck with a fury. I watched as their chairs did cartwheels across the shore, like so many tumbleweeds. Surging waves threatened to float their coolers away. So strong were the gusts that, even though I was in my car with the windows closed, my hat flew off.

Like soldiers diving into trenches to escape an artillery barrage, the birds scrambled to locations secluded from the wind blast. Those feathered fools that tarried risked being pasted against the rock cliffs on the north end of the lake (most likely not their preferred migration destination). Once, I thought I glimpsed a large trout, caught near the water's surface, involuntarily surfing across the tips of the whitecaps. Finally, the sight of a picnic table being propelled toward my car inspired me to hastily depart the premises.

Initially, during the drive home to Harrison, my mood was as grim as the weather. Then, I recalled hearing earlier, within the waterfowl's clamor, the unmistakable symphony of spring. From then on, not even the roar of the concrete-outhouse-fracturing, bluster-guster could muffle that joyous sound in my mind. Nor could it buffet the smile from my face.

Outdoor Misadventures

Nordic Nerd

Cross-country skiing misadventures

For a long time, I emerged from winter in the worst physical condition of the year. Then one day, while watching the winter Olympics on television, the thought occurred that snow sports might solve my winter doldrums. So, I decided to try cross-country skiing. Confident in my gifted athleticism, I saw no need for high-priced lessons. After all, it looked easy enough on television.

Hence, for my first attempt, I drove to a crowded cross-country touring resort. Springing from the car, I quickly mounted my skis, turned to grab the ski poles and, right there in front of God and everybody, fell flat on my butt in the parking lot. I suppose a lesser man would have been embarrassed, but not the "Pride of Madison Street, Harrison, Montana." With supreme composure, I arose and took a deep bow, to scattered applause.

Upon paying the fee at the lodge, I was given a trail map and instructed to draw a "stitz" mark (X) wherever I fell. To my chagrin, halfway around the groomed "bunny run," I was suffering acute writing cramps. Even worse, my initial stitz mark-worthy mishap involved a violent encounter with a lodge pole pine. Fact is while learning to stop of my own accord, I ran into or over just about everything that grows in the forest. Things got so bad that, after one especially destructive outing, I found a note on my windshield suggesting I submit an environmental impact statement before skiing again. Clearly my storied athletic prowess was overrated. Truth is I was a "Nordic nerd."

Luckily, one of my few praiseworthy qualities is blind persistence. Accordingly, after several years, I actually became a passable Nordic skier. With growing confidence, I began trying ever-more challenging trails. My stitz marks became fewer. Then one day my fortunes radically reversed.

While whisking down a steep, winding trail, I looked ahead to see that some fool had built a snow ramp directly ahead. In a flash, my skis were soaring toward the tree tops. The view from the ascent's peak was truly stunning, but not nearly as stunning as my impact with the frozen ground.

Then, through the pain-induced fog, I remembered my brother was skiing down the trail not far behind. Suddenly infused with newfound, perverted vigor, I dragged my bruised and battered body to a spot directly alongside the cursed ramp—and waited. Just as my unsuspecting sibling spied the unavoidable calamity, I bellowed, "SURPRISE!" With eyeballs as big as saucers, he hit the ramp at full throttle. Mesmerized, I watched as the hapless wretch's skis shot heavenward. His trajectory blossomed to an involuntary, twisting-jack-knife from the tuck position. A billowing cloud of snow marked his landing. It was wonderful!

After regaining my composure, I scored his effort an 8 on a scale of 10. Regrettably, in an unpardonable breach of form, my brother's skis had separated just as his head thumped the ground. Rushing to his aid, I was greeted by bitter words declaring that I had, "betrayed my blood of blood." Still, after acknowledging that, had the situation been reversed, he would have done the same thing to me, big bro simmered down—somewhat. With that, we skied for home.

These days, I am no longer able to cross-country ski. However, no one can take away my Nordic Nerd memories—or my brother's. Regrettably, though a forgiving man, he never forgets, and I'm still waiting for the hammer to fall.

Failed Mastery of the Slopes

Recalling the link between extreme speed and extreme pain

Gawking down at the speck-sized ski lodge, the awful realization dawned that I was doomed to slide down a nearly vertical, ice-glazed mountain on a set of slick sticks with no brakes. Very soon, I was streaking downward at an Indianapolis 500-worthy speed. I lost count of the number of times I fell. Impact severity ranged from a full-throttle, full-frontal flop to a rump-rupturing thump. Somehow, I managed to land on every bodily extremity except my feet.

Just the day before, some friends had conspired (with the aid of several inhibition-reducing beverages) to convince me (at age forty-five) to try downhill skiing. According to them, the fact that I had never downhill skied wasn't a problem. Indeed, I was assured that, for someone with my superlative athletic abilities, high-priced lessons would be a waste of money. Instead, my buddies would give me an on-site demonstration, and I would master the slopes before finishing the first run.

Nonetheless, I stridently argued it was my experience that extreme speed goes hand-in-hand with extreme pain. When I went on to confess that I am basically averse to hurting at any level, my determined comrades switched their tactics. From then on, I was subjected to goading taunts and machismo-challenging insults. Eventually, their vocal battering prevailed, and I grudgingly consented to join my "pals" at Big Sky Resort.

After several crowd-pleasing fails, exasperated resort employees fairly heaved me aboard a chair lift. From there, my amigos and I ascended high up Lone Mountain. Then, in another display of less-than-stellar athleticism, I tumbled off the chair lift, and flattened a cluster of resentful women and children. My trusty companions then gave me the promised, five-minute, quasi-skiing lesson before abandoning me with a cheery, "See you at the bottom."

Despite the previously described turbulent beginnings, about two-thirds of the way down the run, I was still alive. Then, suddenly, it felt as though I had fallen into the clutches of a jumbo paint-shaker. While rocketing through the series of sadistically-crafted moguls, my eyeballs vibrated forcefully enough to render me blind. My ricocheting knees whacked my chin so hard that I nearly lost consciousness. Then, just when I thought things couldn't possibly get worse, I sailed off over a vast chasm.

At the highest point of my unscheduled flight, I thought I caught a glimpse of Bozeman, thirty-odd miles north. I also conservatively estimated the vertical drop beneath my skis as rivaling that of Yellowstone Falls. Upon impact, my skis, poles, and numerous articles of apparel blew off like shrapnel. Several death-defying somersaults later, after shrewdly using my chin for an emergency brake, I crunched to a halt.

"Yup, I hear you." The voice from behind startled me. Turning stiffly, I beheld a partially-buried, middle-aged man, scraping packed snow from his goggles. Ironically, the old boy had recently plummeted from the same ghastly precipice with similar grim results. Despite our speed-induced, extreme pain, the kindred soul and I burst into laughter.

Lastly, as if to confirm my failed mastery of the slopes, I fell flat on my face on the bunny run, directly in front of the lodge. With that final indignity, my initial day of downhill skiing came to an end. On the long drive home, I ached, literally, for the day of my inevitable revenge on my "pals."

The Hairy Stick

The story of an improbable discovery

Twenty winters ago, I and two buddies went cross-country skiing on the logging road that parallels Beaver Creek near Quake Lake. It was an ideal day for skiing. So, we strapped on our equipment, mounted our skis, and struck a brisk glide up country.

Despite periodically halting to admire the scenery (aka a spot of heavy breathing), we reached the road's end in about two hours and stopped to eat. There, as our sweat turned to ice, we gnawed on frozen sandwiches with chattering teeth. While thus engaged, each man reminded the others what a swell time we were having. At length, it was time to ski back to our vehicle.

After some discussion, I agreed to take the lead. Inspired by visions of a pepperoni pizza and a sudsy beverage, I soon distanced myself from my companions. While stopped to wait for them, I noticed a dark object protruding from the snow on the trail ahead. At first glance, it looked like a hairy stick. When curiosity got the best of me, I skied toward it. Astonishingly, the "hairy stick" turned out to be a moose leg.

When my skiing partners arrived, I watched with amusement as they hurled their hats to the snow in bewilderment. Fortunately, our vast collective knowledge of the great outdoors soon solved the mystery before us. Having totally missed seeing them on the way up, we now shrewdly noted the nearby shattered trees and abnormal snow accumulation. Hence, we quickly deduced that a small avalanche had occurred at that spot previously. Additional intense brainstorming led us to conclude that the unfortunate beast had been caught in the white torrent and, except for one foreleg (from knee to hoof), buried. None of us had ever seen such an improbable sight. Moreover, we unanimously agreed that the moose's manner of demise gave new meaning to the term, "having a bad day."

Abruptly, one man (likely as a result of oxygen deprivation due to overexertion) announced that the critter beneath us was nothing less than an enormous bull moose. Then, in further evidence of mental disarray, he proposed that we return later, dig down to the animal's head, remove the waiting trophy rack and haul it back to town.

A week later, having abandoned all semblance of good judgment, I was standing next to the hairy stick along with my fellow Nordic nuts. Upon attempting to dig, our group came to the disheartening realization that, at the bottom of an avalanche, snow compacts to a density rivaling reinforced concrete. At that moment, no doubt lesser (saner) men would have quit. Not so the tenacious trio. With a soul-stirring shout of, "cross-country skiers eat their wounded," we commenced excavating.

After burrowing so deep as to require throwing snow over our heads, another grim reality was encountered. We discovered that, contrary to conventional wisdom, the measure between the knee and the top of an upside down, buried moose's head is considerably longer than that same measure on an upright unburied moose. Finally, at the excavation's deepest point, we met with the cruelest reality of all: our prophesied, trophy-racked bull was a furry-headed cow.

From time to time, I still see my skiing companions from that day. Often, the conversation turns to our improbable discovery. In retrospect, all three of us agree that excavating the hairy stick wasn't the smartest thing we ever did. Nonetheless, true to our cross-country skiing spirit, not one of us regrets the experience.

Pedaling Through Paradise

Recalling the perils and joys of mountain biking

About thirty-five years ago, I saw an advertisement for a mountain bike. Here was something I could use to get in shape while satisfying my yearning to be outdoors. So, that same day, I drove to Bozeman and purchased an 18-speed model.

Back in Harrison, I used an Allen wrench to adjust the height of the handlebars and seat. In case more adjustments became necessary later, I put the wrench in my pocket. I then drove to nearby Johnston Road, unloaded my new toy and launched my mountain biking adventure. Soon, I was pedaling down the rough road, savoring the natural high that accompanies exercise.

Then, as I bounced over a sizable rock, the handlebars suddenly slammed down onto the bike's frame. Immediately, the front wheel angled off-center, thrusting my weight sharply forward. Thus did I come face-to-dirt with a grim mountain-bike reality: catapulting over the handlebars and thumping down on a dirt road really smarts. After expressing vocabulary sure to condemn me to the infernal regions, I sheepishly noticed I had failed to adequately tighten the nut that held the handlebars in place. When finished refastening said nut, I reckoned the bent Allen wrench was proof that ample torque had been applied.

That same day, I was desperately trying to maintain control while careening down a steep hill. Just as the bike reached death-defying speed, I ran over a still-steaming cowpie. Upon finally stopping, I was confronted with my second mountain bike disenchantment: "they don't come equipped with fenders!" To my disgust, a stream of bovine discharge extended up the back of my t-shirt, neck, hair and ball cap. Using the unstained side of the t-shirt, I cleaned up as best I could. As a final insult, for the remainder of the ride, I was accompanied by my very own cloud of blowflies. At that point, a lesser man's steadfastness might have wavered. However, there was no way the intrepid Harrison daredevil, "Crash Kehler," was throwing in the t-shirt.

Despite further unfortunate incidents, I eventually got the hang of the sport. The ensuing years provided many unforgettable moments. For example, once I was pedaling on a narrow logging road near Cliff Lake. After blazing down a hill, I rounded a blind corner to discover a cow moose standing broadside on the road. With the brakes locked, I skidded sideways while the astonished, mega-nosed mammal hopped sideways in front of me. With the hair on both our necks standing on end, we stood motionless for what seemed forever. Finally, left with no other option, I flashed the dumbfounded beast my warmest smile and gingerly pedaled past her. Angels actually do watch over fools.

Another day, on the Gravely Range Road, a more lighthearted instance occurred. Because mountain bikes are quiet, I was able to pedal close to a coyote, with its head buried in a gopher hole. Intent on a meal, it had no clue I was present until, with depraved gusto, I bellowed, "SURPRISE!" To my vast delight, the ensuing acrobatics mocked the laws of physics. With no knee bend, the bug-eyed critter rocketed skyward, switched direction in midair and, with furiously churning feet, streaked from sight. Once again, I tumbled from my bike, only that time, due to mirth-induced incapacitation.

Ultimately, there were many other such incidents before I became physically incapable of mountain biking. These days, old "Crash Kehler" prefers to crash in the easy chair and recall the perils and joys of his time spent pedaling through paradise. It's easier on the body.

A Foe Not Soon Forgotten

The story of a memorable day and an even more memorable fish

Slowly twirling across the water's surface, the yellow leaf hinted at the gilded residents lurking below. The scent of molding leaves permeated the crisp air. On that early November day, I was standing by my favorite fishing hole on Willow Creek, a short distance upstream from Willow Creek Reservoir near Harrison, Montana. To my left, a small wooden bridge cast its shade over the pool's deepest part. On the stream's far side, a sunken log extended into those dark depths, thus forming a lair for large trout.

Although I wouldn't have spurned a rainbow, I was primarily casting for spawning brown trout. I was equipped with a weight-forward, sinking fly line tied to a 10-foot, 3X tippet. At the leader's end dangled a large, brown marabou streamer that I had affectionately dubbed "Darth Baiter." After false casting, I laid that feathered bait slightly upstream from the log. I waited until old Darth reached the deepest recesses of the hole. Then, I spun the streamer sharply upstream and began a rapid retrieve. Flicking the rod tip in a series of short, pulsating strokes, made the willowy, marabou tail waggle feverishly. As a result, Darth Baiter tauntingly mimicked a minnow that, having seen a hungry trout, was frantically swimming to safety. For any trout worthy of the title, "game fish," such a blatant challenge is the human equivalent of a slap across the chili-chompers with a greasy, leather glove.

Thanks to the bludgeoning strike, setting the hook proved unnecessary. As the rod tip surged violently toward the water,

I inhaled a startled gasp which caused my jockey briefs to be drawn into a reclusive bodily region seldom visited by cloth. Simultaneously, my teeth clashed together with sufficient intensity to cleanly bisect a lead sinker, and my eyeballs bulged to horsefly-like proportions. Still in the same breath, both feet shot sideways to a wide stance while my knees bent deeply. Thus, in a microsecond, without the aid of a single conscious thought, I had assumed the classic "fisherman's fighting posture."

Abruptly, the heavy fish streaked for the branches attached to the aforementioned log. There was no doubt that if it were able to wrap the leader around those limbs, the battle was lost. So, I leaned back, drawing the line perilously tight. The fray raged to and fro as, like heavyweights trading body blows, we slugged it out for an extended time.

Just when I thought the rod would splinter, the trout changed tactics and lunged for the bottom of the hole. Through the line, I could feel its jaw scraping the stream's rocky bottom as the veteran water warrior tried to dislodge the streamer. Despite the strain, I kept the rod tip raised. By now, it was obvious I was locked in hand-to-fin combat with the aquatic equivalent of a kung fu master. While lightning fast, its every move was fluid, with no wasted effort. It was as though I could interpret the calculated scheming of its mind.

After a period of deep-water parry and thrust, in the blink of an eye, the fish charged downstream. The reel screamed as I applied pressure on the departing line, trying to turn my dogged foe. With strong thrusts of its tail, the trout strained mightily to cross into a downstream hole. Just inches before reaching that goal, it turned and headed my way. The tide of battle had turned.

As my shadowy foe drew grudgingly closer, for the first time, it broke the water's surface. Writhing in the sunlit water directly to my front, the fish appeared as a living bar of gold. Barely fitting my net, I managed to heave the male brown trout onto the bank, where it laid with its gills a-flopping while I lay nearby with my nostrils a-flaring. Shortly, I stretched out my measuring tape. From the tip of his hooked jaw to the end of his tail, the fish measured 25-inches. Arrayed in spawning finery, he was truly a sight to see. The exquisite blends of gold, yellow, tan, brown and red hues were dazzling.

Immediately, visions of triumphantly returning to town, with trophy in hand, danced through my mind. Word travels fast in a small town, and I just knew a brass band awaited me in Harrison. Furthermore, I imagined the town's only sidewalk thronged with cheering citizens while fair maidens scattered marabou feathers in my path.

Then, a sobering thought entered my mind: "This critter and I share a common ancestral homeland." After all, my surname is ethnic German, and he was clearly a specimen of the German brown trout stocked in our continent's waters centuries prior. Thus, I dubbed him "Bismarck." In a further extension of my fertile imagination, I considered that, some two centuries previous, my great-great grandfather, Fritz "Fischersnagger" Kehler, had combated his great-great grandfather in a Black Forest stream. As well, the insight dawned that, if uber-gramps Fritz hadn't released my worthy adversary's distant ancestor, this day's treasured events could never have happened.

In the end, I just couldn't take that splendid creature's life. I placed Bismarck back into Willow Creek, holding him until his strength returned. Then, ensuring his status as a "foe not soon forgotten," with a disdainful swish of his tail, Bismarck splashed water in my face before returning to his lair.

There is no photograph of that fish. No one but me ever saw it. Thus, the band never sounded a note, the crowd never cheered, and no feathers fluttered in the air. However, to me, none of that matters. I will carry the memory of that epic struggle with me to my dying-day. In the final analysis, that trout's unconquerable spirit deserved a nobler demise than a frying pan and a lifeless photo on a wall. "Auf Wiedersehen, Bismarck."

Of Fishing and Snakes

Lessons learned about serpents while fishing

It has been my experience that fishing and snakes just go together. Fact is, I have run into more serpents while trout fishing then at any other time. However, without those encounters, I never would have learned the lessons necessary to coexist with them.

For instance, one day, I was fishing Willow Creek above where it flows into Harrison Lake. Soon, I spied an enticing fishing hole on the far side of a small opening in the thick stream-side brush. The opening was small enough that I had to get on my hands and knees to access it. Nevertheless, I just knew a monster trout was waiting in that secluded hole to attack my streamer with a bone-jarring strike.

Regrettably, visions of an even more stimulating strike loomed when, halfway through the tunnel-like opening, I noticed movement ahead. That movement turned out to be a rattlesnake crawling across the opening close enough for me to spit on. After what seemed like hours, the rattler's buttons disappeared into the brush. I'm not sure if there is an official speed record for backing up while on one's hands and knees, but if there is, I'm pretty sure I shattered it. From that thrilling encounter, I discovered the following:

- From the vantage point of the hands and knees, a rattlesnake looks the size of a boa constrictor.
- When on one's hands and knees, the most convenient target for a serpent's fangs is one's snout.
- Crawling over a rattlesnake for a fish is never a good idea.

On another occasion, a fishing buddy, his dog, and I were walking down a trail leading to the Madison River. The dog was leading the way. Abruptly, I heard a shrill "Yipe!" In a fraction of a second, a furry rocket streaked past me to take up residence at the rear of the procession. Fearless Fido had nearly stepped on a rattlesnake.

Left to defend ourselves, my amigo and I dealt with the enraged serpent. During the ensuing fray, I learned more lessons regarding serpents, such as:

- A fly rod is a poor instrument with which to try to kill a snake.
- There's a chance the snake will strike at the rod and hook itself on your fly.
- If so, convincing anybody to net your catch will be a hard sell indeed.
- Catch and release are out of the question.

On yet another occasion, I was fishing in Beartrap Canyon. After a while, I spied a rock on which to sit. As I rounded said rock, I stepped on a large bull snake. The serpent immediately launched into a belly-up, hissing, twisting, writhing performance designed the scare the crap out of its adversary. The melodrama worked splendidly as I pitched over backward, landed on the far side of the rock, spun on my heels and exited the scene in a disorderly rout. Then, while collecting discarded articles of equipment, I recounted the lessons learned:

- Bear bells are of limited value for alerting snakes of a fisherman's approach.
- Waders aren't well suited for bounding over tall brush.
- It is better to run away today and live to run away another day.

In the end, after serious contemplation, I summed up all my serpent-taught lessons into three golden rules:

ArtKehler

- Snakes don't like it when people step on them.
- People don't like it when they step on snakes.
- Fishing and snakes just go together, so watch where you're stepping.

A Fitting Fit

A lesson in trout fishing etiquette

I have been a trout fisherman since my adolescence. Of all the fishermen I have known since that time, one stands out above the rest. Leo (not his real name) and I became acquainted many years ago when we both lived in the same small town. Because we both worked different shifts at different jobs, we seldom fished together. Nonetheless, when it came to catching fish, we shared an unspoken competition. So, whenever I caught a sizable specimen (20 inches or longer), I made it a point to stop by Leo's house and triumphantly dangle it beneath his nose.

At the sight of each whopper, Leo would invariably yank his hat off, hurl it to the ground, and kick it across the lawn. That dramatic preamble would be followed by great gnashing of teeth, foot stomping, and thrusting of fists into the air. At the same time, he expressed his unrestrained resentment with such colorful assertions as, "I was just fishing that (obscenity) stretch of that (cussword) creek yesterday and didn't catch a (profanity) thing." For his grand finale, Leo would issue such condemning oaths as, "May your pricey, graphite fly rod suffer a compound fracture." and "May your Muddler Minnows muddle through muddy waters."

Of course, every distasteful word was sweet music to my ears. Furthermore, every crude gesture was executed to perfection. What looked like an impromptu tantrum was, in reality, a finely orchestrated, intoxicating spectacle designed to compliment a fellow angler to the utmost. A televised interview on the evening news, with my lunker displayed for all to see, would not have been as rewarding as Leo's selfless act of raging respect.

Eventually, the intense gratification I derived from the old boy's theatrics, caused me to realize how much I was indebted to Leo. After all, any amateur fly-flinger could have said, "Wow. That's a big fish," On the contrary, it took a genuine, dyed-in-the-wool fisherman to recognize the need for ego-enhancing indignation. Obviously, Leo knew how to throw a fitting fit.

Regrettably, as the old saying goes, "Every dog has its day." One day, after I had savored a series of triumphal displays, Leo showed up at my door with a 25-inch-long rainbow trout in hand. In his eagerness to present the trophy for my disapproval, he nearly flopped me in the chops with it. Leo's face could barely contain his beaming, vengeful smile. What else could I do?

With all the artistic flair a mortal man can muster, I whipped off my hat, flung it to the ground, and (utilizing dramatic soccer form) kicked it clean over his car. Then, I boisterously bemoaned the fact that, two days previously, I had "whipped the (bad-word) waters of that very (blankety-blank) hole to a (cussword) lather, without garnering a single strike." Next, with my forefinger thrust heavenward, I called down the wrath of the ghosts of unnaturally-deceased trout all over his greasy fishing hat. Lastly, as a supreme tribute, I retrieved my hat and—chewed on it.

Ultimately, I had to admit the look of bliss on Leo's face was heartwarming, even for me. In fact, I believe I saw a tear of appreciation, glinting in his eye, as he left. The circle had come full round. Leo and I had exchanged fitting fits. The ghosts of unnaturally-deceased trout had returned to their rightful abode. Most importantly, in terms of trout fishing etiquette, all was well again.

Insults across the Waters

Recalling innovative attempts to increase fishing success

Come to think of it, my father was pretty smart. He knew that the average 10-year-old boy has the patience of a Chihuahua with attention deficit disorder. Thus, when he took me fishing for the first time, we went to a small stream brimming with diminutive brook trout that voraciously gobbled anything that dared plop into their watery domain. Within minutes, I had caught my first fish, and have been an avid fisherman since.

Through my adolescent years, small streams continued to be my fishing destination of choice. It didn't take long to discover that fish in such crystal clear waters are extremely wary. Hence, it seemed reasonable to experiment with creative schemes designed to enhance my fish-stalking expertise.

My initial brain-storm involved squeezing juice from night-crawlers into my insect-repellent bottle. By this means, I planned to drive away biting insects while simultaneously attracting trout like iron filings to a magnet. After generously lathering on the odoriferous concoction, I crept confidently forward. Alas, well before reaching the creek, a throng of hunger-crazed birds quickly turned my stealthy advance into a disorganized rout. It was while hastily, jettisoning various articles of fishing gear when I recalled that trout aren't alone in their hankering for worms.

In another burst of intellectual flowering, years before such hats were commercially available, I camouflaged my angling hat using brown and black shoe polish. Initially, I thought I had a winner. Regrettably, one day, an inopportune rain shower revealed a serious defect in my invention. It turns out that, after being doused with water, shoe polish on cloth turns to fluid, which swiftly flows into the eyes, where it assumes the attributes of molten lava. The resulting blind, violent trampling of flora and agonized writhing, in full view of my intended prey, did little to increase my catch numbers.

Yet another epiphany involved tying a small mirror to the tip of my rod and, ever so slowly, extending said viewing device over an inviting hole. By so doing, I planned to locate wily lunkers before casting. To my dismay, I discovered that, because they have no eyelids, trout can't squint. Therefore, when, like a laser beam, ultra-concentrated light is seared into their mega-dilated pupils, they vanish with the speed of a Star Wars warplane. If trout could scream, I'm sure they would have.

Some five decades later, I have come to grips with a seldom-vocalized truth about trout: despite their storied image, they are often so cautious as to be disrespectful. The brutal reality is, there are days when no amount of stealth or skill will entice "salmo-trutta-insolenta" to hand-to-fin-combat.

So, in a radical shift of strategy, I have begun fighting fire with fire. In short, my current response to such rudeness is to hurl insults across the waters. To illustrate, after an hour of unrewarded effort, I begin expressing terms of scolding derision, such as:

- water wimps
- dorsal dorks
- scaly scavengers
- slimy slackers
- finned-bottom-feeders, and
- spineless-speckled-shirkers

If, at the end of the day, the above mentioned modest reproaches have had no effect, insults designed to cut to the quick are launched such as:

- You call yourselves game fish. Ha,
- I shake my unscathed worms in your general direction.
- I rattle my lures toward your lair.
- I flutter my flies at your hideaway.

Other examples include:

- You who snuggle with suckers.
- I've seen lowly carp with more self respect. and
- Your gills suck sluggish waters.

Then, as a final gesture of disdain, I vigorously shake my fist toward the stream, before departing with deliberate dignity. Once, I'm pretty sure I saw a reddish blush rising from the depths.

From the above, one might conclude that I have grown to dislike trout. Never let it be said. Like any enduring relationship, we've had our ups and downs. However, in the final analysis, I can't imagine this world without that splendidly colored, aquatic royalty in it. So, if while fishing one day, you happen upon what appears to be a deranged man, randomly hurling insults at an invisible adversary, take no alarm. It's just old Art, still perfecting his life-long, favorite pursuit.

A Bug Too Big

A rookies' tale of fishing the salmon fly hatch

My first experience fishing the salmon fly hatch took place in the Beartrap Canyon. Early in the morning, I followed a path, paralleling a creek on the canyon's north side, down to the Madison River. Because the spring runoff was at its zenith, I could hear the turbulent river before I saw it. Having never laid eyes on a salmon fly before, I was a rookie in the truest sense.

After arriving at the river's bank, I nearly jumped out of my hip boots when something that felt about the size of a chicken hawk landed on the back of my neck. Instinctively, my hands flailed at the area under attack. Then, while dislodging the mysterious beast, I knocked my fishing hat into the river. When I made a desperate lunge to retrieve it, I fell into the heavy water. Luckily, I was able to reach dry land again with my treasured headwear in hand.

Soon after, while standing next to a willow bush, I had the uneasy feeling that something was watching me. Slowly, I turned my head. Next, I found myself staring, eyeball to eyeball, at what looked like a freakish lizard of the kind one would expect to see in the Galapagos Islands. Convinced the ghastly creature was about to chomp a chunk out of my nose, I summarily retreated.

Upon regaining my wits, I noticed that the surrounding bushes were thronged with like specimens. Thus, I came to the conclusion that the humongous organisms (along with the mysterious critter that had lit on my neck previously) must be salmon flies. Still, to eyes that were accustomed to seeing normally proportioned trout flies they were indeed—a bug too big. Further inspection revealed the salmon flies' pinkish-orange coloration and plump proportions. That observation led me to speculate that trout found them irresistible because they resembled aquatic frankfurters.

As the sun rose higher, the enormous insects swarmed over the river. They floated by in such numbers that the trout, like bowhead whales engulfing plankton, swam with their mouths perpetually open. The fish became so bloated it's a wonder they didn't burst. Consequently, fishing the salmon fly hatch turned out to be problematic.

To begin, due to the weight of the fish plus the effects of the canyon's heavy current, their strikes nearly jerked me off my feet. Moreover, as soon as a large trout felt the hook, it would streak downstream for the Missouri River headwaters. Obviously, putting sufficient line on one's reel would have been tricky. On average, I landed two out of every ten trout I hooked. Still, it was great fun.

After all, what other sporting adventure provides a participant the opportunity to flaunt his equilibrium skills while being dragged two-hundred yards down a river over slimy rocks? Additionally, not many angling exploits offer an angler the thrill of listening as high-priced fly fishing line screams off his reel until he's forced to break the tippet before there's no line left. Lastly, few fishing experiences afford a humbled fisherman the honor of saluting the finned victor still affixed to his disconnected tippet.

Despite its ominous beginnings, my rookie attempt at fishing the salmon fly hatch turned out swell. At the end of the day my arms ached, but I had landed enough large fish to save face. I even survived my initial encounter with "a bug too big". In fact, I look forward to future encounters with them—provided one doesn't land on my neck.

Arctic Angling

Some reservations concerning a popular winter sport

To be honest, I might enjoy ice fishing—if it wasn't for the ice. Even the term "ice fishing" is misleading because people don't fish in the ice; they fish in the water below the ice. And therein, as I see it, lies the problem.

Because humans are heavier than water, the idea of standing atop water, frozen or otherwise, just never seemed overly smart to me. Also, determining the amount of weight a given thickness of ice can support is an inexact science to say the least. What's more, the only way to determine ice thickness is to boldly (recklessly) stride out over the frozen substance and drill a hole in it. Worst of all, if during that process, an ice fisherman (aka arctic angler) discovers the ice isn't as thick as assumed, he could find himself swimming with the fishes. Given such goose-bump-raising circumstances, perhaps I can be forgiven for not hankering to join in the fun.

As well, I question the wisdom of blissfully fishing while, all around me, loud cracking sounds echo across the lake. Nor am I inclined (while being so serenaded) to drill numerous, closely-spaced fishing holes in the already fracturing ice. Most worrisome, such a precarious scenario could result in a classic, "Art Kehler spontaneous retreat," during which, while bellowing, "Out of the way, fools," I would doubtless flatten anything, man or beast, in my path to shoreline safety. Why, I ask, would anyone risk such public humiliation for a couple of stiff fish?

On another less-than-praiseworthy note, it's a proven fact that a trout's metabolism slows down drastically during the winter. As a devoted warm-weather, open-water angler, who relishes fighting fully energetic trout, the idea of catching a semi-comatose fish doesn't seem proper. Likewise, I am not thrilled with using a stubby rod (stunted crane) to unceremoniously yank a feeble quarry through a hole, as quickly as possible.

Then, there's the little matter of temperature. As I see it, ice and frigid weather just go together. Moreover, winter winds, especially when howling across ice, can quickly freeze the toughest arctic anglers to a board-like consistency. That cold-hard fact runs counter to one of my fundamental rules of fishing: "Under no circumstances should a fisherman have a lower body temperature than the fish he is trying to catch."

Lastly, there's the issue of ice fishing houses. I can't help but wonder why a fisherman would want to fish in a house? Obviously, they provide protection from the above-mentioned inclement weather. But then, why venture out into the great outdoors just to stare at four walls? If I wanted to be housebound, I'd stay home.

Still, it must be admitted that ice fishing does provide a way for lots of folks to enjoy hypothermia. After all, it is true that, "A family that freezes together stays together." Also, if it wasn't for arctic angling, occurrences of acute cabin fever would become even more widespread than they already are.

All things considered, not even walking over the ice while wearing an arctic scuba-diving suit with an inner tube strapped around my waist could entice me to give ice fishing a try. The thought of suffering a "spontaneous retreat" while so garbed and having the mortifying spectacle recorded on numerous cell phone cameras, is simply unendurable. Therefore, I think it best for everyone's sake that I keep both my feet firmly planted on solid ground and leave ice fishing to the arctic anglers.

Hunting, Then and Now

The transformation of an old hunter

It was the first day of the big-game hunting season. I got out of bed at 4:30 am and drove to Potosi Canyon, near Pony, Montana. Using a flashlight, I walked through the dark woods until reaching a meadow near timberline on Potosi Peak. At dawn's light, I spied a bull elk grazing about a hundred yards away. I took aim and squeezed the trigger. Soon, I blissfully stared down at the first wapiti I'd ever bagged.

Because the bull was lying sideways on a steep slope, I had to tie the two uphill legs to tree branches to hold the carcass, belly up, while I dressed it out. Suddenly, as I strained to remove the animal's innards, the tree branch holding its upper, rear leg snapped. In a flash, a rock-like hoof walloped me upside the head, launching my hunter-orange hat skyward like a streaking flare. Simultaneously, I was knocked downhill, head over heels. Only by cleverly burying my face in sagebrush, was I able to stop the dangerous descent. Then, while staring down at some bewildered ants, I pondered over who was hurt worse—me or the elk? With my euphoric state shattered, I clawed back up the mountain and finished gutting the animal. Then came the long walk down to the Jeep.

Back in Harrison, certain that they would jump at the opportunity to help drag out my elk, I began calling my many amigos. To my dismay, call after call, the initial calloused response was the same, "And just where's this bulky beast at?" When informed of the remote location, the excuses ran the gamut from, "I'd like to help, but my house is on fire," to "I've come down with a fatal disease." Finally, I found three "pals" willing to help, but only after swearing a solemn oath to, never again, shoot an elk "where mountain goats fear to tread." Aside from frequent disparaging remarks questioning my intellectual capacity, the lung-searing climb back up the mountain proved uneventful. Eventually, we reached the bull and quartered it. Finally, things were going my way.

Later, while dragging my quarter of elk over an icy section of the steep mountainside, the quarter abruptly zoomed forward, striking me behind the knees like a runaway freight train. Once again, crafty use of the cranium saved the day when, just before hurtling over a ledge, I wedged my head beneath a fallen tree. By then, I couldn't help but wonder if the elk's departed spirit was extracting revenge. To make a long story short, the critter I killed at dawn was hung in my shed at midnight.

Today, forty hunting seasons later, this old hunter's hunting methods have changed radically. Fact is I recently bought a digital camera. Unlike the .30-06's triggered recoil, pushing the camera's shutter-release button doesn't loosen any tooth fillings. Unlike the rifle's muzzle blast, the shutter's closure doesn't leave my ears ringing like the bells of Notre Dame. More importantly, the pictures stored on said camera are vastly easier to retrieve from the woods than a large carcass.

Still, when it comes to filling an empty belly, photo prints just don't measure up to a tender, flavorful elk steak. Indeed, the photos' leathery texture and inky aftertaste actually discourage consumption. Moreover, I can't pass my trusty .30-06 without feeling a sense of shameful abandonment. What pains me most is that, unlike after previous successful hunting seasons, I can no longer lord it over hapless hunters who failed to bag their wapiti. Alas, old-hunter transformation is never easy.

The Snake Hunt

The story of a memorable initiation

Not long after having moved to Madison County, Montana, I received a phone call from a friend in Norris inviting me to go rattlesnake hunting. Instantly, I recognized the situation. I was being considered for induction into the Tri-City Fraternity of Prevaricators, Poachers, and Procrastinators. The storied group consisted of local good old boys, whose principal aspiration in life was to hunt, fish, and carouse without end.

As a rule, members weren't prone to study astrophysics. However, they were highly proficient in the more practical skills, like setting a hook without putting your beverage down or blasting a deer from the roof of your house without loosening shingles. Above all, the rough and ready fellows welcomed any challenge, no matter how mindless, to their country-boy image. Clearly my mettle was being tested.

As we drove to the dens, my partner, a charter group member, told of his many harrowing experiences with rattlesnakes while growing up in Norris. Early on, a guy learned to watch where he stepped. However, there were times my buddy was caught off guard. His most galling recollections centered on those occasions when he dashed from home to catch the school bus, only to blunder onto a buzzing rattler.

Invariably, with no knee bend whatsoever, my amigo would vault into what he described as a "spirited jig," complete with twittering toes, flailing extremities, and schoolbooks hurled in the air. Then, as assorted papers wafted down, the humiliated lad endured the howling guffaws of his schoolmates. As he spoke, it was obvious the intervening years had done little to diminish his malice towards rattlers. Nearing the dens, I sensed there was more to the man's dislike of snakes than was rational.

Before long, the pickup rolled to a stop. My companion grabbed his "snake snagger," a wooden rod with an attached wire hoop, which he used to pull snakes from the den. I loaded my shotgun. With my neck hairs standing on end, we tiptoed through the sagebrush and peered at the mouth of the den. Suddenly, my sidekick jubilantly proclaimed that he had spotted the "slimy sidewinders." I watched in dismay as he fairly skipped to the den. Within minutes furious serpents were being dropped on the ground around me. As each snake hit the ground, I quickly dispatched it. After shooting three, I needed to reload.

As I reached for a cartridge, a venomous viper plopped to the ground on my left. I appealed to my cohort to hold up. Unfortunately, by now he was wholly engrossed in snaring the hated antagonists of his youth and, oblivious to my predicament, continued snagging snakes. I fumbled to load the cartridge and shot the snake. As I groped for a new shell, yet another enraged reptile landed on my right. By this time, I was getting a tad tense and dropped the round. Trying hard not to sound panicky, I once more shouted at my comrade that he was getting ahead of me. Again, he failed to heed my request. By the time the next snake flopped to the dirt, it seemed that rattlers were raining down around my ears.

Up to that precise moment, I would have thought it impossible for a man's toenails to scrunch into the soles of his boots with such force as to adversely affect the muscles controlling solid waste discharge. Suffice it to say, only a heroic display of concentrated willpower averted a shameful spectacle. Unable to suppress my emotions any longer, I erupted with a heartfelt verbal onslaught questioning the extent of the old boy's intellectual prowess, casting doubt on his familial lineage and plainly asserting that I was indeed not ready for more snakes.

Jolted from his rapture by my outburst, my partner appeared to be wounded. He responded that he was perfectly willing to wait and added, with an air of dignified aplomb, that there was "no call to be rude." After at last reloading, I shot the remaining snakes and looked to see the dauntless serpent snagger gleefully confiscating more reptiles. I knew then that the man had taken full leave of his senses. It was payback time for all those mortifying mornings and only the demise of the last loathsome serpent would restore his nature.

After what seemed an endless afternoon, I was plum thrilled to see that last snake. Amazingly enough, ignoring every survival instinct, I had somehow stood my ground. In so doing, I had passed the iron test and was admitted to the legendary brotherhood without further ado. Secretly though, I just knew that when the next call came to go snake hunting, something profoundly more important would take precedence, like watching dust fall on my television set.

Bull Elk Bugling Refined

Re-examining a time-honored tradition

Not long ago, I had the pleasure of talking to an old friend about bugling for bull elk. I had never tried my hand at bugling and so, found the conversation very interesting. I was surprised to find out that my buddy had taught himself to bugle. I was even more impressed when he detailed the innovative process by which he learned.

As I listened intently, he described how, after buying a bugling device, he also bought an audio tape of bull elk bugling in the wild. Then, with his store-bought bugle, the novice would sit in his easy chair and try to imitate the taped sound of real bulls in the rut. Next, he utilized what I consider to be a uniquely innovative idea.

Upon reaching a level of proficiency that warranted judgment, the crafty experimenter asked his wife to go into another room of their house and listen. Then, in random order, the taped bugles would be played, interspersed with his efforts. Thus, his trusted mate could render her frank opinion on how his efforts compared to the real thing.

After many such sessions, the good wife proclaimed that she could no longer differentiate between the genuine bull elk bugles and his bugles. Thereafter, my friend felt confident to trumpet wapiti rutting taunts and dares across the wilds. I have to admit I couldn't help but admire the old boy's ingenious yet simple methods.

However, following due deliberation, I perceived a flaw in his methods. In particular, I took exception to the idea of sending a woman into the listening room. No offense to the ladies but, only a fellow male (hereafter referred to as the buglee) can react appropriately to the rut-induced, personal insults of another male critter. For that reason, as I see it, use of a buglee provides a more accurate measure of bugling progress.

For instance, say one day while listening to the bugler's taunting calls, the buglee is suddenly overwhelmed by primordial stirrings. Consequently, with his neck muscles bulging, the buglee charges from the listening room. Snorting furiously, he then wrenches the bugler from his chair, and delivers several bone rattling head butts before power slamming the poor wretch off the nearby wall.

At that triumphant moment, there can be no doubt that the erstwhile bugler's artistry has attained a whole new level of proficiency. Even more gratifying, if upon regally exiting the premises, the buglee marks his turf on the front door, the battered bugler can take supreme comfort in knowing that he has achieved bugling perfection.

Still, despite my considerable contribution, it was my old pal who developed the original, imaginative process. Far be it from me to steal the thunder of such a deserving bull elk bugler. Hence, I feel it only fair to award him the opportunity to test my alteration first. Generous soul that I am, I'll even volunteer to be the buglee. I'll keep ya posted.

Mighty Poor Dumplings

A bird hunting story of yesteryear

Several decades ago, on the day before the opening of upland bird hunting season, I encountered a recent acquaintance. We struck up a conversation and, before long, agreed to hunt grouse (aka prairie chickens) in the fields around Harrison. Early the next morning, I pulled into his driveway. As the young man approached, I noticed that he was carrying a .22 caliber rifle. Trained in the exalted sport of wing shooting, it had never occurred to me to hunt game birds with a rifle. While climbing into my Jeep, I noticed him skeptically eyeballing my 20-gauge shotgun, leaning against the seat. An awkward quiet ensued as we headed for the fields.

Soon, I turned onto the Old Yellowstone Trail. We hadn't gone far into the first field when six feathered heads suddenly poked above the stubble. My hunting partner watched as I strode toward the prey, scattergun at the ready. With each step, the prairie chickens' spindly necks grew longer. Finally, they exploded into flight. I swung on the lead bird and snapped the trigger. The 20 gauge cracked, and the grouse nose-dived to the ground. If I dare say so myself, the whole dramatic scene was as close to poetry in motion as any mortal is ever likely to see. As a variety of down, plumes, and quills drifted downward, I awaited the flowery profusion of compliments sure to follow such a splendid performance.

Instead, to my dismay, my companion loudly proclaimed, "What in blazes did you do that for?" Then, he gruffly declared that anybody with a lick of sense knew grouse were supposed to be plunked in the noggin before they fly. The words struck like a dagger to my heart. I replied that shooting birds on the ground was an intolerable affront to my sporting sensibilities. My cohort countered that watching supper being blown to smithereens offended his dining sensibilities. With jaws set and necks bowed, we glared across the stubble. After a tense moment, I retrieved my prairie chicken, and we moved on.

When next we spotted targets, I watched the marksman do his thing. I had to admit he was a crack shot. Still, it seemed to me like cold-blooded assassination, bereft of sport. Aside from an after-dinner belch, I questioned what possible fulfillment could be derived from such sordid behavior? He wondered if it were not equally sordid to take home a grouse that rattled when shook? Wounded to the core, I countered with what I thought was a foolproof argument. "If your sole intent is unsullied meat," I demanded," then why not do away with any pretense of fair chase and simply pounce on the hapless creature and strangle the life out of it?" Dismissing my line of reasoning as being "over-the-top," the sharpshooter stuck to his conviction that the whole idea of bird hunting was to collect the fixings for a grouse stew. "And," he smugly concluded, "bb's make mighty poor dumplings."

Grudgingly, I had to admit the rifleman had acquitted himself well in the exchange of verbal body blows. With neither of us willing to concede, an uneasy truce settled over the proceedings. At the end of the day, the prairie chickens were dutifully separated into piles of "murdered" and "mutilated." Then, with his bevy in hand, the young man disappeared into his house.

Over the ensuing years, the emotions of that long-ago-day have softened. Recently, when I encountered the sharpshooter in Harrison, he admitted that he still "plunks a few in the noggin." Deep down, I can't blame him because he is right—bbs really do make "mighty poor dumplings."

Memorable Misadventures

Recollections of less-than-ideal hunting excursions

Like many Montanans, I've endured some less-than-Ideal hunting excursions. For instance, there was the morning I was hunting with a companion near Norris. Before long, my partner shot a deer not far from Pony Gulch. After dressing out the buck, we attached a rope and dragged it to the rim of the gulch. Always eager to minimize exertion, my companion opted to shove his critter over the rim and let it slide to the bottom. Noting the steepness of the slope, I retreated from the edge a short distance before cautioning him to be mindful of his footing.

When launched, the carcass streaked downward. Regrettably, the young man had failed to notice he was standing on the knotted, loose end of the drag rope. Thus, when the rope drew taut, his right foot was yanked from under him. In a flash, my cohort vanished from sight.

Within seconds, the top of a small pine tree, that rose just above the rim, whipped violently downward and then ricocheted back. Presently, the most dreadful groan ever to besiege my ears rose above the gulch. Concerned, I raced to the rim's edge and gaped down. Not twenty yards below sat my blue-faced partner, straddling the still quivering tree. Clearly it was not the time to say, "I told you so."

Meanwhile, far below, the deer's carcass bounced indifferently onward. Only after a reassuring, physical self-examination was the shaken hunter able to recover the deer. He spoke with a noticeable soprano lilt for some time after.

Another misfortune happened in the Camp Creek area,

near Potosi Canyon. While hunting the woods for elk, I stepped over a sizable fallen tree. Lo and behold, just as my lead foot ascended the tree's far side, a hulking cow moose rose up mere feet away. The hair on the back of her neck stood on end as steam from her nostrils blew past my ears. With my .30-06 still slung, had the situation turned violent, I wouldn't have had time to shoot. As time stood still, my life flashed before my eyes, and it wasn't a pretty collage. Finally, to my immense relief, the cow stormed off in a huff. Subsequently, I resolved never to forget, "Moose don't like surprises."

Yet another mishap transpired when I was hunting with a friend near Sterling. The morning was cold and snow was falling heavily. After reaching the desired location, I parked my white, full-metal cab Jeep in a meadow. As was customary, we struck out in opposite directions.

After an hour of fruitless effort, I turned back toward the vehicle. About half-way, I encountered my pal. He announced that he had bagged a large buck deer and breathlessly recounted the details of the stalk and kill. Then, he nonchalantly mentioned that the critter had frozen stiff while being dragged. So, instead of forcing it into the back of the cab, my pal had stood the rigid, five-point buck alongside my snow-white Jeep, in the midst of a snow storm and departed.

Instantly, I imagined successive hunters, thrilled at their good fortune, blasting at what appeared to be a large buck standing in a snow-covered meadow. I also envisioned my treasured Jeep perforated with gaping bullet holes. A spirited discussion regarding the merits of intelligent forethought ensued as we hot-footed back to the meadow. Just as we reached the still unscathed Jeep, a truck appeared on a nearby hill. No doubt misadventures such as those described above are cause for angst. Nevertheless, they also make less-than-ideal hunting excursions memorable.

Bear Dilemma

Imagining a bad scenario

A number of years ago, in mid-May, I was walking up the dirt road to Cataract Lake behind Pony, Montana. Steeply inclined, it was one of my favorite conditioning routes. Within minutes, I was breathing heavily enough to suck pine cones from the nearby trees.

Approximately a hundred yards before reaching the top of a ridge, a steep forested gully pressed next to the road. Because I was aware that bears were out of hibernation, before traversing past the gully, I checked to ensure that my bear spray was fastened to my belt. Then, the thought occurred, "What would happen if a bruin actually did stroll onto the road twenty yards ahead?" As I pictured said critter, I realized that a vigorous wind was blowing directly into my face.

Over the years, I have noticed that bear spray producers aren't eager to advertise the negative effect strong winds have on their products. The grim reality was that, at that moment, spraying toward my imagined adversary would not have proven unbearable for the bear (no pun intended). Instead, a distressing portion of the fiery fluid would have been propelled backward, engulfing my unappreciative snout and eyeballs. Thereafter, while I thrashed in agony, the beast could have feasted at its leisure. Obviously, that would not have been an ideal outcome.

As a young man, I served in the Army. Consequently, when confronted with dangerous circumstances such as the above imagined, I tend to think from a military perspective. Regrettably, I have to admit, my initial idea to, "call in an air strike," was not well thought out. However, upon further contemplation, I reckoned that two opposing strategies would offer the best chance to preserve my weathered hide.

Strategy one would have involved dashing past the startled predator to gain an upwind advantage, from which I could spray with abandon. However, this tactic posed a challenge. The road I was climbing was quite narrow with a high bank on the uphill side and a steep drop-off on the downhill side. That said, in order to prevent being toppled off the road, the hairy beast and I would have to pass in such close proximity as to necessitate a brief, yet unavoidable clinch. Surely, we both would have found that predicament awkward to say the least.

Strategy two involved its own set of challenges. Obviously, a panicky, disorganized rout would have triggered the animal's predatory instincts. Therefore, a better course of action appeared to be a slow, dignified withdrawal, while at the same time, hurling intimidating threats. I refer to such warnings as: "Don't let two seconds of courage ruin the rest of your life, fatso." and "Come on ahead, make my day, carrion breath." One could hardly blame a bear for losing courage in the face of such bravado. But then, what if the animal was hard of hearing?

Just then, another blast of wind snapped me back to the present. I blotted the picture of the imagined bruin from my mind and bravely plodded safely to the crest. Hopefully, there will never be a need to test either strategy.

Ultimately, time spent thinking is never wasted. Since that day, I have conjured up an idea to develop a portable, light-weight, bear spray, grenade launcher. Said device, would propel a canister of the fiery substance that would burst upon contact with contentious bruins. In that way, walkers will be able to avoid awkward clinches and other such bear dilemmas. I'll keep ya posted.

Autumn Perspectives

Dealing with contending perceptions of my favorite time of the year

Who knows, perhaps it is because I am getting older and more jaded. At any rate, of all the seasons of the year, I previously considered autumn (fall, Indian summer) to be the most idyllic. However, that treasured viewpoint came under question when, while conducting a dispassionate scrutiny of my favorite time of the year, I encountered a less pleasant perspective.

For example, rather than being serene, fall is a contentious time of the year. The woods fairly reverberate with boisterous sounds. Ruffed grouse tauntingly thump their wings on fallen trees. Bull elk hurl crude insults at one another. Mule deer bucks lock horns in neck wrenching battle. With rude grunts, bears gobble every edible thing in sight to pack on weight for hibernation.

Also, in our streams, brown trout combat the currents to run upstream, where the male fish bash into the females as part of a violent spawning rite. Following close behind, rainbow trout fight the same currents to pitilessly devour the brown trout's freshly laid eggs—a favor sure to be returned come spring.

As well, out on the prairie, barely mobile rattlesnakes sullenly slither past grateful rodents, toward their dank dens. With bruising body slams, antelope bucks thwart any attempts by wayward does to escape their harems. While developing patches of white fur, jackrabbits become especially vulnerable to stalking coyotes.

Additionally, up on the alpine peaks, bighorn rams repeatedly try their best to bash each other's heads in. An early snowstorm coats already harrowing mountain goat trails with treacherous ice. Overhead, sounding a final good riddance, geese wing south with nary a backward glance.

Most dismal of all is the fate of the deciduous tree leaves. For a period of about a month and a half, due to incremental chlorophyll reduction, they slowly strangle. Then, in a cruel climax, the leaves' seasonal transformation ends with a death spiral. So much for idyllic perceptions.

Still, there's just no denying that the leaves' brief reign of kaleidoscopic color trumps all off-putting aspects of fall. Their dazzling array is fully capable of mesmerizing one's senses. As such, it is obvious that any attempts to dispassionately scrutinize Indian summer are doomed to fail.

Therefore, this year again, no doubt, I will fall prey to autumn's spell. Multi-hued leaves, hanging from the trees and carpeting the ground, will still rouse within me visions of color gone mad. And, once more, the sweet musky aroma of the rotting leaves will prove to be intoxicating.

As a result, just as in years past, I will be moved to take off my shoes and socks and, in my bare feet, trod over what appears to be a magic carpet. Then, as the cool, damp leaves ooze between my toes, I will doubtless reunite with a virtually forgotten bond that exists between soul, sole, and sod. There is an unmatched gladness in the act, a gladness which I am certain will overwhelm any contending perspectives and reinstate my perception of autumn as idyllic.

An Undying Resentment

Unsavory facts concerning an unpleasant creature

One day during March, while walking on my lawn, I noticed that various bushes were beginning to bud. Despite the scattered snowflakes fluttering to the ground, that undeniable sign of spring produced in me a feeling of euphoria. Regrettably, that night my elation was cut short when I observed another sign of spring hanging from my arm: a wood tick.

Over my lifetime, I have encountered a number of parasitic life forms. I can't say I'm particularly fond of any of them. However, among those bloodsucking creatures, only ticks have earned my undying resentment. Following is a list of unsavory facts that, I believe, support my bitter attitude toward ticks.

Unsavory fact #1: Ticks are devious. Even doing a body check, showering, and inspecting one's clothes aren't always enough. I've had the crafty critters lie in wait overnight in my car seat and, like the evil reincarnation of Star Trek's, "Return of the Klingons," bushwhack me the next day.

Unsavory fact #2: Ticks are gluttonous. Unlike mosquitoes that gulp their reasonable quota and leave quickly, ticks are in it for the long run. Once, I had one hang on for days. During that time, it gorged itself to such hideously bloated proportions that the repulsive parasite resembled a raisin with legs. Unsurprisingly, after that, Raisin Bran cereal was not on my menu for some time.

Unsavory fact #3: Ticks have no respect. Often as not, they have attached themselves to bodily locations I was unable to reach. However, most despicable by far were those ticks that dared to burrow into highly classified anatomical territory. They cared not a whit that their obnoxious intrusions bordered on the scandalous. The ghastly images nearly caused me to hyperventilate.

In such extreme cases, my dignity soon fell by the wayside. I was compelled to have the shameless invader removed by a medical professional, sworn to doctor-patient confidentiality. Even then, remaining motionless while said hypersensitive regions were probed with sharp-edged tweezers required nerves of steel. In an attempt to prevent permanent psychological trauma, I was reduced to offering bribes to be rendered unconscious for the entire procedure.

Unsavory fact #4: Ticks are gross. I didn't mind sharing a little of my blood from time to time, but it's what was done with that blood that grieved me. The gruesome truth is that, after a female tick had stolen my blood, she used it to fertilize her eggs. Words could not express my disgust at discovering that my vital fluids were spawning a brood of mini vampires. Now that's gross.

Unsavory fact #5: Last but not least is the sobering reality that some ticks carry Rocky Mountain Spotted Fever and Lyme disease. So, it's not enough that a tick had already encroached on my personal space, hounded me relentlessly, stayed too long, scandalized my sensibilities, humiliated me, and grossed me out. The vile bug also had the potential to render me grievously ill.

In the end, I believe the above-presented unsavory facts fully validate my undying resentment toward ticks. I guess there is an ecological reason for the euphoria-shattering creatures, but for the life of me, I can't imagine what it would be. In fact, on the day when I (hopefully) ascend to the pearly gates, despite the risk of appearing irreverent, I may well take this unsavory list along and ask, "Why?"

Harrowing Hiking

Reminiscences of some spine-tingling trekking experiences

It all began when my dad first took me into the mountains. I was so young that he led me by the hand. As we progressed, Father pointed out the many eyes observing us: a squirrel peeking around a tree, a shadowy brook trout watching from a tiny stream, a deer peering through thick brush. Those things, along with the smell of the woods, proved irresistible. Thanks to Dad, over the next five decades, I hiked more miles than I can begin to estimate. Following, are two of my many harrowing hiking experiences.

To begin, there was the time I climbed to the top of Hollowtop Mountain in the Tobacco Root Mountains. The day was so clear I could see the MSU Field House in Bozeman with my naked eye. Shortly, I edged over to the south side of the mountain, where it drops nearly vertically for hundreds of feet. The scenery was spectacular. Standing on that precipice, I felt alone with the mountain.

Abruptly, a high-pitched whistle (scream) pierced the air. The raucous sound was so deafening it seemed that whatever creature was responsible for it had been perched on my hat. Severely stunned, I lost my balance and began twirling my arms wildly. While teetering on the edge of disaster, I endured a "breathtaking" (in the truest sense of the word) view of Mason Lakes far below. Finally, I fell backward to safety. Right then, with my heart still slamming against my Adam's apple, I vowed revenge on the dastardly beast that had nearly caused my demise.

After considerable scrutiny, I spied a small animal on a

rock about twenty yards away. It seemed impossible that such a pint-sized, pipsqueak could muster such a humongous noise. Nevertheless, the alpine windbag soon launched another shrill performance, confirming its guilt. Then, I realized I had just encountered my first American pika.

Despite the preceding spine-tingling events, I had to admit the furry little stubby-eared, rabbit-like critter was one of the cutest animals I had ever seen. Even so, had I been able to get my still-shaking hands on it, I would have severely restricted the summit soprano's capacity to vocalize.

Yet another harrowing trekking event happened when I was hiking in the Madison Range south of Ennis. Because the path was steep, I was breathing heavily. As a result, I was looking down at the trail, instead of looking ahead. For just a moment, I forgot Dad's long-ago lesson concerning observing eyes.

Suddenly, I heard a loud "woof" and heard timber crashing directly to my front. I had surprised a bear. Intent on survival, I reached to grab my 357-magnum revolver from its shoulder holster beneath my right arm. As spine-tingling seconds passed, I continued to flail wildly at the weapon. Then, to my immense relief, I spied the bruin retreating through the woods. It turned out to be as petrified as I was. Lastly, to my mortification, I noticed that I had nearly torn off my shirt sleeve, without ever having extracted the pistol from its holster.

Upon arriving back in Harrison, neighbors asked what happened to my shirt sleeve. Desperate to save face, I told them it got shredded when the bear tried to grab my pistol from its holster. I was promptly laughed to scorn. Ultimately, I had no choice but to reveal the humiliating truth. The next day, I bought a can of hip-holstered bear spray.

Wild Game Meat Cutting Memories

A few clever cleaver stories

Many years ago, I operated a meat cutting shop in Harrison, Montana. During hunting season, I routinely arose at 6 am and cut game until midnight. Young and full of vinegar, I actually enjoyed the work. Some memorable wild game processing events occurred during that time.

Most notable was an incident involving five hunters from a mid-western state. As was often the case, those particular "hunters" were in Montana more to party than to hunt. One day after a morning of merrymaking, the lads decided to go for an afternoon hunt (aka drive around on dirt roads with guns). Nearly exhausted by the effort, the eagle-eyed fellows finally spied a mule deer buck standing on top of a ridge, just as the sun was going down.

Like an elite SWAT team, the five men erupted from their jeep and instantly began blazing away. The ensuing barrage nearly caused an evacuation of nearby Pony. Though wounded, the animal managed to cross over the ridge and descend the far side before expiring. By the time the wily trackers jockeyed their jeep to the ridge top, the sun had set. Then, while searching for the buck through the tall sagebrush, they ran over it with the jeep.

Bursting with pride, the lads dressed out their trophy and forthrightly hauled it to my shop. While peeling off its hide, in addition to the unsightly tire marks, I counted nine bullet entry holes (most of which were in non-vital regions). The wretched creature had been shot from every direction except overhead. It was the only deer I ever hung from hooks that rattled when shook.

Midmorning the next day, the marksmen strode into the shop with broad smiles and breath that could pickle a roll of salami with a single exhalation. They proceeded to instruct me on precisely how to process their critter. Choice steaks were to be 3/4-inch thick. Roasts were to be a certain weight etc, etc. With saintly restraint, I listened until they'd finished before blurting out, "That deer looks like it suffered a direct hit from an 81 mm mortar. You'll be lucky to get 10 pounds of hamburger from the mutilated beast." The hurt look on their faces still bothers me.

Another memorable event took place when a young man came to the shop with the first moose he'd ever shot. While inspecting the animal, I noticed the bull was so old his beard was gray. Having cut such specimens previously, I mentioned that the meat might be a just tad chewy and a trifle dry. So thrilled was he at his accomplishment that the greenhorn failed to pay attention.

Nonetheless, I earnestly tried to tenderize the meat. I ran the boned-out steaks through an electric cuber-tenderizer. Next, I pounded them with a wooden mallet until my hands went numb. Still, the steaks retained the texture of weathered moccasins.

Directly after sampling a steak, the disenchanted moose-flesh connoisseur returned to the shop. Aghast, he recounted how, after twenty minutes of strenuous chewing, not only did he sprain his jaw, but the chunk of steak he was endeavoring to devour grew to twice its original size. Plus, the meat was so dry that, in order to restore his shriveled tongue, the young man had to message it with Bag Balm—repeatedly. Some folks just don't listen.

Alas, such are the fond memories of a retired, wild-game meat cutter. I must admit, I enjoy reliving them in my mind. Like fine wine, they only get better with time.

The Art of Aging Gracelessly

Blossoming Phase

An untraditional view of aging

Like everyone else, during my life, I have transitioned through various phases of development: infancy, childhood, adolescence, teenager, and so on. Personally, I have long believed that, especially as they pertain to my own life, such traditional labels lack sufficient clarity. For instance, in contrast to "infancy," I prefer the "diabolical-diaper phase." Similarly, rather than "childhood," I consider that innocent time as the "double-dare phase." Likewise, "adolescence" is more aptly expressed as the "notorious-nerd phase," and my time spent as a "teenager" best described as the "pimpled-punk phase."

Of late, it dawned that I had entered yet another distinct phase of my life. As expected, none of the traditional labels fittingly described what had transpired. For instance, the title "elderly" seemed premature. However, neither was the designation "middle aged" any longer appropriate. And so, it became necessary to conjure up another suitably candid label.

Obviously, retirement played a part in my transformation. Still the realization occurred that aging wasn't the only agent of change. What mattered more was that I had clearly experienced a dramatic physical and intellectual enhancement. Consequently, I dubbed my new state of being the "blossoming phase."

Indeed, physical blossoming began when the ravages of time significantly restricted my ability to exercise. Equally damning, was the fact that I had not mastered the science of perpetual fasting. Together, these new circumstances created the perfect storm for physical blossoming of a sort thus far unknown to me. Whereas, in my younger days, such blossoming referred to increased muscle mass, this time it related to enhanced girth mass. If things keep trending as they are, my tailoring needs will soon require the skills of Omar-the-tent-maker.

As for intellectual blossoming, it came about after retirement. To be honest, previously, I can't recall ever hearing my name and the word "intellectual" spoken in the same sentence. Nonetheless, with time to contemplate, I recognized that I possessed a lifetime of experience. Further, in a mysterious leap of understanding, I suddenly realized that experience, when combined with the fog of age, turns to sparkling intellect. That empowering enlightenment resulted in an irrepressible need for me to bless as many folks as possible with my sage-like wisdom. Thank goodness I am no longer able to tackle people on the street. I even had to suppress the urge to call strangers on the phone and ask if there was anything they needed to know. Things got so bad that I took to having my pearls of wisdom published. In that way, folks who might have otherwise escaped my learned counsel were subjected to it over their morning coffee.

Ultimately, for a man previously acclaimed for his modest-to-a-fault demeanor, this current condition has left me disillusioned and more than a little embarrassed. Instead of a return to youthful brawniness, I have been left looking like the Pillsbury Doughboy. The ballyhooed explosion of smarts has led to threats of incarceration for "assault and blather." Still, in the final analysis, there's no denying this new phase did spark an enhancement—of sorts. That aside, here's hoping my "blossoming phase" has done bloomed, and I can rejoin the ranks of unmodified folks—in both body and mind.

A Pain Named Frank

Striding through a twisted situation

I remember that morning, twenty-six years-ago, as though it were yesterday. A splendid day awaited me as I sprang from the bed. Then, as I bent over to pick some clothes off the floor, I felt my butt suddenly plunge downward and slide to the right. In rapid-fire sequence, my toes seized the carpet, my teeth clenched, my eyelids slammed shut, and both ears snapped back against my skull. Every muscle was so taut that wiggling my toes ruffled my scalp. Instinctively I shouted, "My back's gone out."

Gingerly reaching for the phone, I made an appointment with the local doctor. Just getting to the car proved challenging. With my spine twisted, both knees bent sideways and my right foot hovering an inch off the ground, I advanced in erratic, compact circles. The drive to the doctor's office seemed interminable.

Following a brief exam, the general-practitioner confidently announced, "Yup, your back's out." Strangely, I was not greatly comforted by the old boy's keen powers of observation. Muscle relaxants were prescribed. Additionally, I was instructed to stay moderately active. I protested that any level of activity resulted in misery. The doctor responded that I should ignore all discomfort except for "frank" pain. Being a stickler for clarity, I demanded that he describe "frank pain." The physician, a man of surprising candor, then described said pain as, "any hurting severe enough to result in upward curling of the toe nails and profuse sweating of the teeth."

Regrettably, that enlightening day proved not to be the

last occasion when my back went out. For a while, I sought the services of chiropractors. Whereupon, large men performed aerial gymnastics on my back, for which they had the audacity to send me a bill. Usually, after enduring three weeks of their legal assault, my back felt better. Then, one day, following a particularly vigorous (barbaric) treatment, I set forth to develop a more genteel means of self-treatment.

The first step in my remedy for sudden-skeletal-slippage involved accepting the fact that, although the prospect held a certain appeal, I wasn't going to die. Having assuaged my fears, I then decided that I would stride my spine back into alignment. Admittedly, walking soon after my spine had gone astray proved immensely unpleasant. I commenced in a twisted, bent gait best described as the "Cro-Magnon trundle." My feet barely cleared the ground, and each swaying shuffle was accompanied by a primordial grunt. In keeping with the mood, I found it helpful to carry a hand-hewed, wooden spear for balance. Surprisingly, after trekking so for half an hour, my knuckles ceased dragging on the ground. With spirits soaring, I grittily trudged on and soon could assume what I called the "Neanderthal lurch." After an hour, I was actually able to resume the posture of a contemporary human being.

Of course, the second I sat down, my vertebrae would again go out. However, with continued effort, I was eventually able to begin walking in the "Neanderthal lurch" position. Amazingly, in three weeks, I was actually capable of starting out in the traditional stride of a modern man. In the process, I also saved considerable money.

Over time, sudden-skeletal-slippage and I became pretty tight (pun intended). As a result, I learned that pain hurts, and frank pain really hurts. I also discovered that not everything that hurts is bad, all thanks to a pain named Frank.

Sharp as a Marble

Dealing with a disturbing tendency

Recently, I've noticed I have developed an alarming tendency to forget things. In fact, I have been reduced to listing all the things I have to do each day. Even then, I neglect to do half of them. This morning was a prime example. I was supposed to meet some friends at the local restaurant for breakfast. At the appointed time, I left my house, locked the entry door, and started my car. Then, I remembered I forgot the mail I wanted to drop off at the Post Office. Frustrated with myself, I shut off the engine, unlocked the entry door, and retrieved the letters. After restarting the motor, I recalled I had forgotten to put on my driving glasses. While muttering under my breath, I repeated the process all over again.

At long last, I arrived at the café—ten minutes late. When the first person greeted me, despite having known him for years, for an embarrassing moment, I couldn't think of his name. To make matters worse, as I struggled to comprehend what was being said, I realized I had forgotten to put in my hearing aids. Sadly, I wasn't the only one in our group to do so. Needless to say, the conversations were both boisterous and repetitive. At times, I forgot what I was saying in mid-sentence. Fortunately, I have learned to change the subject of a sentence so seamlessly that no one even noticed. We discussed everything from the stock market to scours—at least I think we did.

When it came time to leave the cafe, I asked for a doggy bag. Then, I paid the bill, wished everyone a fond adieu, and drove home. As I opened my house door, the phone rang. The café was calling to remind me I had left my doggy bag on the counter. Needless to say, the return to the restaurant was not a shining moment.

By then, I was not only embarrassed, but honestly concerned about my inability to recall things. Desperate for reassurance, I sat down and recorded the following things I'm still sharp as a marble at remembering. Invariably, I don't forget to:

- breathe
- sleep
- wake up
- blink
- yawn
- put my feet on the floor before attempting to walk
- open my mouth before speaking

On an even more advanced cognitive level, I also always remember to:

- never offer an honest opinion concerning the actual appearance of a newborn child
- never feed a visiting pal's dog chili, cheese, and onions before he takes the mutt home in his car
- never announce my arrival at a psychiatric ward by dropping a metal garbage can lid on the concrete floor
- never put a whoopee cushion on an electric chair

As might be expected, after completing the above impressive lists, I felt much better. Also, as I thought about it, I concluded my problem was not forgetfulness at all. Rather it was because, these days, I am more easily distracted from my line of thought. At any rate, that rationalization sounded more palatable. Perish the thought that anyone might think I'm losing my mind—such as it is.

The Abhorrent Utterance

A hard-learned lesson in dealing with the legally lethargic

A while back, I and some other retired gentlemen of leisure volunteered to do a small construction project in a local community park. As tools and materials were being loaded into pickup trucks, the communal mood was so merry that humming could be heard. Before long, boards were being measured, cut, nailed together, and put into place. Having been a carpenter when I was much younger, it actually felt good to be doing construction again.

Then, a younger (not yet retired) volunteer showed up to help. Initially, his appearance was greeted with enthusiasm. However, before long, the obviously naïve, thirty-something man committed the cardinal sin as it relates to operating with retirees. Without the slightest consideration for whom he was dealing with, the insensitive brute referred to what we were doing as—WORK!

Instantly, a clearly audible gasp reverberated through the park. The abhorrent utterance rendered our previously merry band momentarily immobile and speechless. Fully conscious now that what was being done constituted physical labor, our spirits waned perceptibly. A gray pall engulfed the proceedings.

For the first time, the harsh realization dawned that both the tools and the materials being used were heavy. Consequently, every action became odious. We also became aware that the job involved lots of bending and, worse yet, straightening up again. Shortly, the afore-mentioned humming was replaced by strained grunts and groans. Even more discouraging, everyone began to sweat profusely from doing the same job we had been enjoying just a few innocent moments before.

At that point, the inarticulate culprit recognized his appalling social blunder. As a result, he tried to express regret, but it was too late. The irreparable psychological damage had already occurred and all attempts to right the grievous wrong were met with icy stares. As was fitting under the circumstances, over the next three grueling hours, the poor wretch endured a veritable cascade of verbal chastisements.

Obviously, I can't speak for my fellows. However, the following morning, I felt the weight of everyone of my sixty-nine years, plus a decade or so. My spine was as stiff as a shovel handle. My shoulders throbbed and my hands were totally numb. It hurt to comb my hair. Even my breath was labored. And the cold hard fact was that, if the dreaded "W" word had been spelled out instead of fully spoken, the experience wouldn't have been nearly so traumatic, and I wouldn't have felt so miserable, but—NOOO!

As I think back on it, it's a marvel our band of genteel pensioners was able to bear up. Indeed, it wasn't that we were adverse to reasonable physical exertion. It's just that we had long ago paid our laboring dues during our many years of gainful employment. Accordingly, having now attained the exalted status of legally lethargic retirees, we've chosen not to describe what we're doing as "work"—EVER. Call it an endeavor, a project or even a task and there's no problem. Just don't use the "W" word.

In the end, it must be admitted that, despite his abhorrent utterance, the naïve brute's skillful contributions were beyond substantial. The finished product wound up looking pretty good. Here's hoping he took his hard-learned lesson in dealing with the legally lethargic to heart. I'm not sure this pensioner would survive another such traumatizing event.

Dubious Compliments

Recollections concerning the art of aging gracefully

A few years ago, while walking the streets of Butte, I glanced at the person approaching me on the sidewalk. At the same time, he glanced up to see me. We both stopped in our tracks. If anyone had been listening closely, I am sure they would have heard the sound of two aged minds grinding furiously.

What followed was one of those awkward moments that folks my age (67 at the time) too often encounter. Instinctively, we both assumed a feet-spread-wide, knees-bent-outward, hands-poised-at- our-sides stance that suggested an Old West style gunfight might break out. For what seemed like several minutes, we eyeballed each other from a distance of about ten feet.

Finally, the old boy spoke up: "I think I know you, but I don't know from where, and I can't remember your name either." Embarrassingly enough, I had to confess my recollections of him were equally uncertain. Still, we both sensed that our paths had indeed crossed in the distant past. Even so, I couldn't recall if we had been friends or adversaries at the time. (I never claimed to be a saint).

So, while still retaining a defensive posture, we warily began exchanging the names of places where we had worked, and people we had known over the years. After a while, our life stories began to connect somewhat. With that, the mutual mood relaxed to the point where we felt confident enough to reveal our identities. Regrettably, even hearing the other guy's name didn't ring a bell for either of us.

Suddenly, the mystery man blurted out: "Now I remember.

You're old Hammer Slammer, ain't ya?" Recognizing my nickname from the 1970s, I abruptly remembered him, and replied, "Yes I am, and you're Michelob Mick, right?" Immediately, frowning expressions were replaced with wide grins. Hearty handshakes quickly followed. As it turned out, we had worked together as carpenters for a short time in Big Timber.

Then, as so often happens when older gents meet again after forty years, the conversation went awry. I began by expressing the expected compliments regarding his appearance while, at the same time, saying to myself what I really thought.

"You look great" (Egad, this guy looks like a botched attempt at taxidermy.) "You haven't aged a bit" (I've seen dried cow pies with less-conspicuous wrinkles.) "You look as though you could still put in a hard day's work" (He couldn't stack marshmallows.) "Your language is as colorful as ever" (He sounds like a belch from beyond the grave.)

Of course, when I'd finished showering him with obviously insincere accolades, he responded in blatant kind. The signs of deceitful speech were clearly evident: the barely suppressed gasp of shock at my appearance, the inability to look me in the eye while spewing his dubious compliments and his forced smile. Certainly what transpired was a charade, but then, we both knew it was better than hearing the brutal truth. All in all, I reckoned it was a finely-orchestrated exercise in the art of aging gracefully.

Upon parting, Michelob Mick and I agreed not to wait another forty years to meet again, which made sense because, by then, chances are we'd both be dead. When all was said and done, I had to admit it was good to see the old boy. Despite its tentative beginnings, our encounter had brought back many memories, even if they were dubious.

Return to Quiescent Stirrings

One man's method of adjustment to retirement

Smoke from Dad's Chesterfield cigarette drifted through the beam of morning sunlight that shone across the room. Having finished breakfast, my father and I were sitting quietly at the kitchen table. It was the summer of 1958. When Pop took another drag on his cigarette, I casually mentioned that, in six short months, I would be old enough to hunt small game. Continuing that line of thought, I expressed my sincere concern that it just wouldn't be fitting if his adoring son had to go hunting with a hand full of rocks. Awaiting dear-old Dad's reply, visions of a gift-wrapped, new shotgun, lying next to my birthday cake, flashed in my mind. Instead, I recoiled in horror at Pop's blood-curdling reply, "Well then son, I guess you'd better get a job."

My desperate pontification detailing the evils of child labor fell on deaf ears. As a result, I grudgingly found a job delivering newspapers. Every day of the week, twelve months of the year, I staggered from bed at the ghastly hour of 5 am, to slog the nearly nine miles of my paper route. Through snow, rain, sleet, wind, and dogs that mistook me for an animated chew bone, I persevered. However, as a reward, enough money was saved to buy that shotgun. Additionally, in a stunning turn of events, the job actually proved to be enjoyable. Work provided me with a hitherto unknown sense of pride and purpose, which proved beneficial during the following extensive period of adult labor.

Some fifty-four years later, I retired from the ranks of the toiling masses to join the legions of the legally slothful. However, the realization soon occurred that rocketing from bed at the crack of noon and loitering for the rest of the day could never make me happy. And so, I chose to view that watershed event as the launching of a writing career. Other endeavors would include helping neighbors less fortunate than me and becoming more involved in community activities. Hence retirement wouldn't require radical lifestyle change.

Nevertheless, there was one long-relished rite of passage, which simply could not be denied. At the end of my last work shift, using a 16 lb. sledgehammer, I smashed my alarm clock to smithereens. Memories of mornings commenced with my fingernails and toenails gouged into the bedroom ceiling quickly propelled my frenzied hammering to a sordid state of rapture. When I couldn't swing anymore, the shattered remains were diligently swept into a dust pan and deposited into the metal barrel in the yard. There, after having liberally doused the cursed remnants in flammable fluid, my gleeful fingers dropped a match. Lastly, as inky smoke spiraled upward, I executed a feverish, Cheyenne shaman's dance, counter-clockwise, around said barrel while calling down the demons of darkness. With that incomparable indulgence finally accomplished, it was time to turn the page.

Currently, I have begun earnestly designing my, "age-appropriate-awakening apparatus." To begin, I propose to fasten my coffee maker, pre-set to activate at 6:30 am, to the cabinet that sits beside my bed. Thus, my slumbering ears shall be serenaded to awareness by the soothing burble of brewing java. Beside said coffee pot, a small fan will be placed and programmed to engage when the ebony elixir is brewed to perfection. Consequently, the titillating aroma of freshly-made coffee shall be, ever-so-gently, wafted across my quivering nostrils and fluttering eyelids. Then, while still semi-comatose, I shall have but to roll over, insert a straw into the pot and leisurely sup the fruit of the blessed bean of bloating bladders to the bloom of full cognizance.

In a further attempt to ensure gradual rising, I am presently searching for a time-programmable, telephone answering machine. On it, plans are to record a message that automatically replies to any call before 7 a.m. with the salutation, "THIS BETTER BE GOOD." After three offenses, the foul perpetrator will be treated to a mega-decibel, responsive call featuring a 105-mm cannon blast immediately followed by a trumpet sounding reveille—at 3 am.

All in all, it is my unselfish intent that my pioneering ideas provide inspiration to other retirees on their path to blissful mornings. Pondering upon it, the thought occurs that, if those efforts prove successful, my life will have come round. I shall have returned to the practice of quiescent stirrings, savored during the days before my father's grim proclamation. In truth, I look forward to my retirement days as being some of the most productive and satisfying of my life—just not before 7 am.

Goofy Juice

Reflections on the perils of poorly considered remarks

Back in the 1978, I underwent my first surgery. The operation required significant slicing and sawing on the back of my neck. When I awoke in my hospital room, the only thing I knew for sure was that it hurt even to raise my eyebrows.

Before long, a "friend" arrived to check on my condition. Renowned for his lack of tact, the old boy took one look at me and blurted, "Egad man, I've seen better looking heads on a zit." After blessing him profusely for his candid observation, I began clamoring for a mirror. To my horror, upon gawking at myself, I discovered he was right. My grossly swollen neck resembled that of a Black Angus bull in the rut. Further, because I had lain face-down in a round rubber mold for several hours, my nose and mouth were encircled by what looked like a toilet ring. In short, my head looked like a wart on the end of a pickle. Just then, the surgeon stopped by to inform me that I would be up and walking the next day. Between the lingering pain and concern about walking so soon, I didn't fall asleep until 4 am the following morning.

Precisely at 5:30 am, a clearly sadistic nurse woke me to tell me that breakfast would be served at 7 am. Oozing sarcasm, I retorted, "How thoughtful of you. This way, I'll have time for a rousing game of tennis before the morning meal." To calm my agitated state, she gave me a shot of pain medication (aka goofy juice).

Within minutes, the world was a bright and wonderful place. Such was my state of euphoria that I began insisting on getting up and walking right then. When told my uplifting wasn't scheduled until the afternoon, I raised an even more boisterous caterwaul. Shortly, in accordance with my request, the hospital staff began prying me out of bed.

At a maximum of 1/32nd of an inch above the pillow, my head felt as though it was going to explode. By the time my toes touched the floor, my previous heroic proclamations had been replaced by such poorly considered remarks as, "Take it easy, you thugs." and "What are you people, barbarians?" Lastly, I endured an excruciating forced-march down the hallway, during which time I emphatically countered each repetition of "no pain, no gain," with "no pain, no stain." Despite such impudence, I was returned to bed without mishap. Ten days later, I walked out of the hospital a wiser man—or, so I thought.

More recently, I underwent a rotator cuff operation. Before the surgery, I was given a sedative. Then, the surgeon stopped by and asked if I had any concerns. I responded, "I'm not worried, doc. I used to be a meat cutter. I've hacked on lots of shoulders, so, I have a pretty decent idea of what you're going to do." Clearly taken aback, the physician replied, "Well, that's certainly an unusual analogy. Thanks—I think?"

It was then I realized that, despite my previous ghastly experiences, I had allowed the goofy juice to obtain control of my tongue again. Consequently, I had just insulted a surgeon immediately prior to going under his knife. Thankfully, the good doctor proved not to be spiteful.

Over the years, I have been fortunate to encounter medical professionals who forgave my poorly considered remarks. As I grow older, I can only hope that trend continues. One thing's for sure. Despite its perils, I'm not likely to pass on the goofy juice.

From Guru to Geezer

Championing the return of an ancient tradition

In ancient times, when a man turned fifty years of age, he entered upon the most revered part of his life. After all, life was brutal in those days and, for a man to reach fifty was a remarkable achievement in itself. Obviously, the old boy had to have more smarts than the average Archimedes or Jehoshaphat. As such, fifty-plus gentlemen were considered not only honored elders, but also a priceless source of wisdom.

Garbed in finely woven robes and leather sandals, such men were not required to soil their hands in common labor. Work was the realm of the young. Instead, these learned fellows strode about with scrolls of parchment tucked beneath their arms as fair maidens sprinkled rose petals in their paths. In short, these guys were the earliest "gurus." The scholarly ones often situated their homes on precipitous mountainsides so as to require laborious exertion, on the part of the seeker, in order to attain their services. Then, the younger members of society approached these aged wonders in awe, to pose questions concerning the deep mysteries of life.

For their efforts, the young would be blessed with such astute adages as: "Never petteth a burning dog, my daughter" or "Never grabbeth a poisonous serpent by the tongue, my son." Rightfully struck dumb by the rarefied knowledge, the grateful young ones would proffer expensive gifts and slowly back away, bowing repeatedly. Upon returning to the valley, they would fairly sing the praises of the enlightened one. For many centuries, this time-honored ritual ensured the continuity of human civilization.

ArtKehler

Oh, how the mighty aged have fallen from gurus to geezers, in the blink of a millennium. Somehow, the population at large has lost sight of the experienced man's lordly presence. At a time in life when I should be dispensing accumulated pearls of wisdom, I continue to toil as a common peasant. Each day, I watch the world scurrying past, as though I am a barely perceptible shadow lurking in a dim corner. Rather than being honored as a "guru," I am considered a "geezer," which translates into modern terminology as: "hopelessly outdated old fart."

Indeed, one cannot deny that, nowadays, due largely to technological innovation, the human environment changes almost daily. We live in the era of the Internet, You Tube, My Space, cell phones, camera phones, iPods, texting, and twitter, to name just a few current communication raves. With those facts in mind, it seems reasonable to assume that an obviously dated specimen such as me could hardly tender any thoughts of contemporary value.

Balderdash, I say. I am, after all, a man whose life has bridged the span between quieter times and this age of ceaseless interaction. Therefore, methinks now may be the perfect time for this "ripened flatulence" to take up the mantle of his honored predecessors by reflecting on some timely observations.

To begin, for what earthly reason would anyone want to establish a page on the Internet on which to post their daily personal happenings to millions of strangers? Isn't old-fashioned neighborhood gossip sordid enough? Should laws be needed to prevent cell phone conversations while steering a four-ton deadly weapon through traffic? Isn't it obvious a vitally more important task is at hand? What's more vital, a camera phone or the right to privacy? What percentage of mobile telephone conversations is actually necessary? Is

"Twitter" a misnomer for "blither?"

With the preceding notes in mind, my age-enlightened counsel is as follows: "For heaven's sake, put a lid on it, my harried children. Blather thy lips far less and listen a great deal more, my son. Twitter thy digital gums far less and observe much more, my daughter." How difficult it is to learn when one never ceases talking, my progeny. Purchasing what is not indispensable in order to do the unnecessary, rewards only insidious commercial advertisers, my victimized children. Abhorrence of anything that forces stillness is, in fact, a frantic attempt to avoid facing one's self, oh you who have forgotten. Each moment spent in pointless busyness is like a breath passed, never to return, my beloved sons and daughters."

In sum, I hope that the above thoughtful advice hastens the return of the guru. Obviously, there is a great need. It is my fondest dream that fifty-plus men will, once again, don robes, sandals, and take up parchment to assume their rightful regal role. Perhaps most importantly, generous gratuities for wisdom dispensed will again justly unburden these worthy souls of undignified labor. Doing so will enable their restoration from the status of gaseous geezers to grand gurus. Oh and one last adage: "Fairest maidens, never tosseth fake rose petals lest offended guru smote thy devious fingers."

Blasts from the Past

The Pugilists

The manly art of self defense defiled

I was born in a rough and tumble mining town. Like many such communities, there were copious personal disputes. As a result, kids fought each other, mothers fought over their kids' fights and fathers fought just because. Fans fought over football games, choirboys fought over hymnals and girl scouts fought over their cookies. Don't get me wrong. At core, these were good people, it's just that they were gravely lacking in the social graces.

Having grown up in that environment himself, our father decided early on that if our teeth were to survive the fourth grade, it would be good for my brother and me to be versed in the manly art of self-defense. An accomplished boxer as a young man, Dad was a skilled instructor. So, at a tender age, we began our pugilistic apprenticeship.

Religiously, every Tuesday evening, my brother and I were led into the living room. Furniture was moved to form a space for boxing. After having slid on gloves bigger than our heads, Pop would bark instructions. For many hours, the brothers Kehler practiced weaving, bobbing, foot movement, jabs, hooks, uppercuts, etc. Over in the corner, Mother stood apprehensively by with cotton swabs and damp towels.

Truth be known, neither my brother nor I inherited our Dad's natural flair for the sweet science. However, what we lacked in finesse was made up for with fervid spirit. Surprisingly, as time went by we actually got passably proficient. Pop beamed with pride watching his budding pugilists in action. Before long, the evenings would proceed to the steady rap-a-tap-rap of measured blows landing in a polished manner.

Sadly, soon or later, the moment Dad dreaded most would arrive when, to everyone's astonishment, one or the other of us would actually manage to land a rousing punch squarely on his adversary's nose. A robust blow landing most anywhere else was rewarded with a complimentary, "good shot." However, there was just something about a stinging, eye-watering thump to the snout that was an unbearable affront to personal honor. An awkward silence would ensue as the ungrateful recipient clutched his throbbing beak. In short order, the wounded warrior would shout, "why you dirty..." At that, my brother and I would crash to the floor, kicking and gouging. To blazes with rules. An urgent, primal need for vengeance overwhelmed any pretense of custom. All semblance of form would evaporate as my brother and I, with gloves now discarded, thrashed about on the floor, choking each other purple. Meanwhile, Dad pleaded, "No-no-no! That's not how it's done."

Try though he may, Father never did convince my brother and me to alter our unrefined ways. Just when he'd think that he had finally gotten through to us, we'd end up on the floor again in another unsightly display. Eventually, Pop came to the rueful realization that neither of his boys was likely to become anything resembling a ring legend.

One day, Dad's cherished boxing gloves mysteriously ended up in the garbage can. It seems that Mother had tired of stuffing cotton in bloody noses and pumping air back into deflated stomachs. Although she didn't come right out and say it, I'm pretty sure Mom also fretted over damaged brain cells her boys could ill afford to lose. Father, fearsome man though he was, never said a word. Not surprisingly, both my brother and I did find success on our school's wrestling squad. It did, however, take the coach a while to persuade us that choking was against the rules.

Universal Language

Memories of a notable morning

My earliest memories of my paternal grandfather took place during my pre-school years. Times were hard, so he was living with my parents, my brother, and me. His given name was Victor, but to our family, he was, "Pap."

One morning, Pap and I were home alone. He was frying himself some eggs, while I was eating a bowl of cereal. In front of me, on the kitchen table, were a milk carton and pencil. For reasons known only to the six-year-old mind, I decided to poke the pencil through the carton, pull it out and watch the milk stream from both sides.

There I sat, silently watching those sparkling, ivory jets arching gracefully through the morning light. Transfixed, I gaped in awe as the creamy puddle slid across the table, to land on the floor in flaring plops. Soon a startled shout shattered my rapture. From his strident tone, I sensed that Pap didn't share my ardor for the scene's aesthetic splendor.

Though English was his primary language, my granddad also spoke German. He firmly believed that, of the two, German reverberated more convincingly when yelled. Thus, whenever Pap lost his temper with me, I was rebuked in a foreign tongue, which didn't particularly bother me, because I didn't understand a word he said. Fact is, despite our "language barrier," I found the dramatic scene entertaining.

First, Pap's eyebrows would rise in dismay. Next, the veins in his neck would bulge, and his face would turn red as a scalded lobster. Then, while shaking his bony finger in my face, Granddad's voice would swell to a bellowing crescendo.

Always he began with the phrase, “Hyleig donnerwetter! Nein, nein, ist verboten!” (Holy thunder weather! No, no, it is forbidden!) From there, Pap would work himself into a lather of righteous indignation, spewing forth ever-more picturesque language. His voice rose and fell with the measured flow of an operatic virtuoso. Every theatrical gesture was performed with polished expertise. There’s no denying, the man was a linguistic impresario in the finest sense. After weathering his tongue-lashing, I was dismissed to conjure up my next caper.

However, this morning was different. This morning there was to be no language barrier. After spying the milk spouting like a Roman fountain, Pap’s eyes narrowed to slits, and he headed straight for me. Instinctively, I sprang from the chair, shot through the front door, streaked across the porch, cleared the steps in two hops, and hit the sidewalk at full throttle.

Certain I had left Pap behind, I smugly glanced over my shoulder. Instead, I watched the old geezer clear those stairs in a single bound. With newfound urgency, I switched on the afterburners and fled down the sidewalk. Just when I thought I’d gotten away, I was captured.

Tucking me under his arm, Pap carried his kicking, squalling grandson back to the kitchen. After a rousing thump up-side the head, I just couldn’t wait to clean up the mess I’d made. Now that I realized Pap’s grip on his emotions was tenuous, we entered a new phase in our relationship. Simply put, he told me what to do, and I did it.

Years later, my grandpa and I recalled that notable morning. I jokingly contended that our language barrier was the root cause of all the unpleasantness. Confirming the power of “universal language,” Pap concurred, replying, “Yep that thump up-side the head said it all.”

Haphazard Headwear

Candid thoughts concerning former hats

One day recently, I noticed the headwear hanging on my hat rack. There was a hat for every season and occasion. That observation led me to reminisce about the many forms of headgear that have graced my pate over the years.

First to spring to mind was my childhood Mickey Mouse ears. Though young, I was fully aware of how dorky I looked when wearing them. Even so, I didn't care. Why? Annette Funicello, that's why. At the time, I had such a crush on Walt Disney's mega star Mouseketeer that, if she had worn a bed pan on her head, I would have done likewise. As I saw it, any girl who could manage to look dazzling while sporting a set of rodent ears was extraordinary.

Then there was the elementary-school dunce cap that, thanks to a cranky English teacher, once crowned my cranium. The injustice of that act of public ridicule troubles me to this day. After all, what mere mortal, after being jolted from a mid-period snooze, would know what the first letter of the alphabet was? Worse yet, based solely on that flimsy evidence, my future claims to intellectual flair were openly questioned.

When compared to current models, my little league football helmet was a primitive skid-lid. So far as inside-the-helmet padding went, a player's hair was considered sufficient cushioning. Given the current controversy concerning football-related concussions, I'm pretty sure I now know the cause of the afore-described dunce cap fiasco.

Unlike today's kids, when wearing a ball cap, I was smart enough to realize that, when I walked, the back of my neck wasn't facing forward. Furthermore, it was common knowledge back then that, positioning the cap's brim precisely centered over the nose, helped maintain balance when skipping on icy sidewalks.

Adorned with dry flies, previously chewed bubble gum, dried night crawler slime, tootsie rolls, and splotches of fish innards, my green fishing beanie (with a flexible band above the rim) was a stream-side fashion statement. Better still, it set the standard for fishing fedoras that both looked and smelled like a part of the natural ecosystem.

Conversely, my first hunting cap was best described as an "Elmer Fudd" hat. Like the headgear worn by Bugs Bunny's old cartoon nemesis, the heavy wool apparel was larger than my head. From a distance, my neck seemed to have blown an orange bubble.

Despite the fact I only wore it for a day, my high-school graduation cap remains unforgettable. On that long-awaited day, some bright spot decided to hold the graduation ceremony on the football field. Naturally, shortly into the procedure, rain began to fall. Next, to my chagrin, the corners of my square shaped, flat-topped graduation cap warped steeply upward. Suffice it to say, it's difficult to be perceived as an educated person while a mini-pagoda sits atop one's skull.

Before every surgery, I was thoughtfully fitted with a shapeless hairnet. In that way, afterward, I was assured of not only appearing as though I had been run over by a truck, but also looking as though my noggin had sprouted a mushroom. Once, striving for a European flair, I purchased an Irish ragamuffin wool hat. Not only did it look like a dry cow pie wavering atop a swollen potato, it also made my already fat head look flat.

Currently, my favorite sombrero appears as an ordinary outback hat. In fact, it's actually an orthopedic hat designed to take the point off my head, caused by wearing all those previous hats. I wonder if Annette would have approved.

Pit-Talk

Memories of an unorthodox method of articulation

Being very young at the time, I don't remember my first haircut. However, my dad assured me that I had been a brave little guy—right up to the instant the barber grabbed the scissors. According to Pop, that ominous action convinced me I was about to have my throat cut. Consequently, I raised a caterwaul that reverberated for the length of the block. After surviving that hair-raising, initial ordeal, I actually began to enjoy my trips to the Mr. Bartonelli's barbershop.

By far, my hometown's largest employers were coal mines. Therefore, many of Mr. Bartonelli's customers were underground miners. Due to regional poverty, the large majority of those men were forced to drop out of school before graduating, in order to help support younger siblings. I never met a miner who didn't smoke or chew tobacco. Hence, the barbershop floor was lined with judiciously-placed, brass spittoons (aka cuspidors). It didn't take me long to observe that the tobacco chewers were excellent shots. A missed attempt drew a stern glare from Mr. Bertonelli. Continued sloppy slobbering risked shunning by the coal crackers' fraternity, a lifelong stain (pun intended) on a member's repute.

During my middle-school-age haircuts, I began to recognize that there was more going on than random spewing. Once I got past the unsavory aspects of tobacco chewing, I began to notice links between the language skills I was learning in school and the dialogue taking place at the barbershop.

To begin, the simultaneous, communal insertion of a fresh chew signified that organized discourse was about to commence. Soon, the "pit-tuey" sounds of tobacco juice being launched and striking its target, echoed throughout the shop. Upon continued observation, I realized the miners, were using "spittoon-tones" as punctuation marks. A delicate blend of chew proportion, velocity, and contact-tone indicated whether the punctuation mark represented was a comma, exclamation point, question mark, period or simply heralded a dramatic pause. Following are a few examples:

- "Yup, 'pit-ting' (comma) old Lefty was one heck of a blaster 'pit-tang' (period)."
- "True enough 'pit-ting' (comma), but it's a shame he blew his right hand off before old Lefty got the hang of it 'pit-thunk' (exclamation point)!"

A particularly resonating spittoon-tone, in the midst of a sentence, was a call for temporary silence. The dramatic pause signaled the announcement of an important event. Naturally, such a momentous effort required a generous chew proportion and a robust launch at a slower rate of speed. Following is an illustration:

- "Word has it 'pit-whomp' (dramatic pause) the miners are going on strike next week 'pit thunk' (exclamation point)!"
- A terse response, in the form of a question, would be designated by a less voluminous discharge at a significantly higher velocity, such as:
- "Say what 'pit-whack' (question mark)?" "Have they gone daft 'pit-whack' (question mark)?"

Thus, through the clever use of an unsavory habit and an equally unsavory receptacle, the supposedly, unsophisticated coal crackers concocted an unorthodox articulation method that overcame their limited schooling. Further, the colorful dialogue demonstrated a level of structure, flow, meaning, and drama difficult to achieve through written language.

In the end, I became proficient enough at understanding "pit-talk" to serve as an unofficial interpreter for the occasional, non-mining-affiliated customer. To this day, I admire the old spittoon-specialist. They said what they thought and meant what they said "pit-thunk!"

Chaotic Christmas

Recollections of a tumultuous holiday long past

It is the first Christmas I clearly remember. Long before dawn my brother and I sprang from bed and fairly shot into the living room. There, to our delight, stood a glowing tree with wrapped presents stuffed beneath it. Then, my brother lunged toward the tree.

Inexplicably, at the same instant, my left foot zipped in front of his right leg. The resulting nasty fall left my sibling sprawled on the floor, just short of the gifts. Aghast at his misfortune, I paused for all of one-quarter of a second before diving beneath the tree. There, I seized the largest present my greedy little arms could encompass and sprinted for the center of the room.

Unbeknownst to me, in the midst of the frenzied action beneath the tree, I had managed to wrap the light cord around my ankle. As a result, upon my gleeful emergence, I pulled the Christmas tree over on top of me. Presently, I was yanked free with a candy cane wedged up my nose and tinsel dangling from my neck. Incredibly, I was still doggedly clutching the treasured present. Obviously, I did not yet grasp the meaning of Christmas.

Over and over I wailed: "I bwoke da Cwismas Twee."– "I bwoke da Cwismas Twee!" Mother's sincerest efforts at consolation fell on deaf ears. I had just suffered the most devastating calamity ever to befall a pre-schooler and nothing could breach the depths of my despair. Of course, my sibling was of great solace with his ear-splitting lament that his little brother had "ruined Christmas forever."

Before very long, I heard my father calling to me: "Hey Buddy, look." At first, my eyes were hesitant to revisit the horror I had perpetrated, but Dad persisted. Forcing myself to look through stinging tears, I stared in disbelief. How handsome was our Christmas tree. Righted again, it stood more majestic than previously. Even my brother ceased his piteous ranting.

Then, with a measure of calm finally restored, our family began to unwrap presents. Without my even noticing, the peaceful, loving spirit of the season soon permeated the room. Things became so harmonious that, when informed that the large present I had previously swiped from beneath the tree belonged to my brother, I returned it without a fight. Even more shocking, when my brother and I both received cap pistols, we put off the inevitable shoot out until the next morning.

After all the gifts had been distributed, I became aware of the decorations on the tree. I noticed that, upon its crown, stood a silver angel. From its branches hung shiny balls of many colors, candy canes, tinsel and, for reasons known solely to Mother, blue lights. Ultimately, despite the day's chaotic beginnings, it was Mother's choice of lights that was to prove most memorable.

Some sixty years later, the sight of blue lights strung on an evergreen still sends my thoughts racing back to the time "I bwoke da Cwismas twee." That's as it should be. After all, it was on that day I first grasped the concept that it's "better to give than to receive." True, that which I gave was my brother's present to begin with, but nonetheless, I did give it back.

Gridiron Glory

Some football blasts from the past

Recently, it dawned on me that football season was upon us. As I contemplated that fact, the sounds of cracking helmets and pads, echoing from the past, recalled my own gridiron experience. Beginning with little league football, my biggest hindrance was my size. Simply put, when I was little—I was little. On the field, I looked like a giant snail shell with attached tenny-runners. Consequently, I was far down on the linebacker's roster. Nevertheless, I diligently showed up for every practice and tried my best. Then one day, it was time for the real thing.

Regrettably, as the season's final little-league game progressed, my team fell further and further behind. Things got so embarrassing that even our parents tactfully exited the stadium. Near the end of the fourth quarter, our coach became so desperate, he put me in the game. At last, here was my opportunity to shine.

Apparently, the other team's coach noticed my diminutive stature because he immediately called the dreaded "student-body right" play. So, when the ball was snapped, the entire opposing team ran to the right and straight at me. Like a true linebacker (idiot), I stood my ground. Consequently, at least half the rival team ran over the full length of my prostrate body. The last kid (the ball carrier) paused long enough to perform a stutter-step on my chest before sprinting for a big gain.

The next thing I remember seeing was my coach staring down at me incredulously. With his chubby jowls shaking back and forth, he loudly proclaimed, "Damn that was gutsy kid—not real smart, but gutsy." My long-awaited gridiron debut was over in a single play.

Still, to everyone's amazement, I grew up to be a starting linebacker on my high school team. To be a varsity linebacker was to be godlike. Pretty cheerleaders spoke your name in hushed tones. Police officers held doors for you. At the local ice cream parlor, extra syrup was conspicuously ladled on my chocolate sundaes. Obviously, football was serious business in my hometown.

In fairness to the coaching staff, they did occasionally make token reference to good sportsmanship. However, more often, we were taught that, "an illegal block is only illegal if it's poorly executed." A hit rendering an opposing player comatose was cause for a standing ovation. Piling on a downed ball carrier was considered teamwork at its finest. The linebacker's creed held that nothing was more disgraceful than a linebacker returning to the huddle, without having hit anyone. Hence, our motto was, "If all else fails, hit the referee."

Surprisingly, my most treasured gridiron memory had nothing to do with tackles for loss or intercepted passes. Rather, it occurred after, on two separate occasions during the same game, an opposing player blind side-blocked me out of my shoes—after the whistle had blown. Swearing revenge, I waited until I spied the devious degenerate standing idle, after a play. At my blind side impact, his helmet flew off like a popped wine cork. Hearing his every vertebra crack in rapid succession, and the great whoosh of air that erupted from his lungs, was nigh on to rapturous. To this day, that stellar episode remains one of the most gratifying moments of my life.

Then a sharp shoulder pain (likely a remnant of the above-mentioned collision) drew me brusquely back to the present.

As I staggered to the medicine cabinet, other assorted football-related injuries made their presence known. Reaching for the Extra-Strength Tylenol, my visions of gridiron glory swiftly faded.

Buck Privates of Life

The pros and cons of sibling status

Just ask anyone who was in the Army, and they'll tell you that a buck private is the lowest life form in its ranks. Roaches are accorded more respect. Buck privates are invariably assigned the most undignified tasks imaginable and are subject to belittlement while they're at it. Their opinion is never sought, and if anything goes wrong, it's always the buck private's fault.

Along those same lines, I have heard it said, "little brothers are the buck privates of life." Having been both a little brother and a buck private obliges me to testify to the shocking parallels in the treatment endured by both. Indeed, my lower-than-a-roach familial rank became all-too-apparent when I was only seven-years-old.

One winter day, my brother (older by two years) and I went sledding on the street that passed by our house. Anxious for adventure, we virtually yanked our only sled up a steep hill. At the summit, I expressed my opinion that I should steer. The very idea of an inexperienced runt like me presuming to think he was capable of guiding our full-sized Red Glider down the hill left my larger sibling aghast. Assuming a haughty, Napoleon-like demeanor, big bro went on to proclaim that obviously, only his steady, veteran hands were worthy of steering the sled. Hence, my opinion was dismissed as mindless drivel. Worse yet, I was assigned the undignified, buck-private-like task of lying on top of him, in the dreaded "slingshot" position.

In no time at all, we were speeding downhill. Halfway down, I became concerned that, rather than advancing toward the middle of the street, "Napoleon" seemed to be headed for a parked car. Drawing closer, I could see we were approaching the car's rear tire. Suddenly feeling like one of Custer's doomed recruits, I braced for the worst. At the last second, I lifted my head for a final peek. Just then, the sled struck the tire, dead center.

Because he had a death grip on the steering handles, big bro was able to control the severity of his impact. Not so little bro, being on top, I had no stabilizing device to grip. Hence, true to the slingshot position's dreaded reputation, I was violently slung frontward.

"Whap," the nauseating sound of a face impacting a convex-shaped hubcap reverberated through the neighborhood. I felt my malleable features melding with the semi-pliable metal. An eerie silence ensued as snow slowly settled around the awful scene.

Finally upright, I gingerly felt my face for evidence of disfigurement. Meanwhile, I overheard my sibling laughing hysterically at the image of my grimaced face left hammered into the hubcap. Even that appalling example of buck-private-like belittlement was trumped when he announced that by hitting the tire he had kept us from gliding into an intersection and thus saved my life. As a final insult, big bro swore that it was my idea to go sledding in the first place. In other words, the entire misfortune was my fault.

To this day, my brother and I hold contesting views of that day's events. Still, his calloused, disrespectful deeds (along with countless similar subsequent examples) did prepare me for the military. As it turned out, life as a buck private in the Army was easier than life as a little brother. Nevertheless, I have yet to thank him.

Old-school Mentoring

Recalling the paternal tutors of my youth

Recently, it occurred to me how much I owe to the men of my Dad's side of my family. Their old-school style of mentorship during my formative years was crucial to my learning. The first example occurred when I was still a preschooler. One day, while my paternal grandfather was reading the morning paper at the kitchen table, I was irresistibly drawn to the shiny coffee pot on the stove. Just as I was about to touch it, Grandpa, without raising his voice, said, "You'll burn your grubby little finger." Being at the age where children need to discover things for themselves, I proceeded to do as I had intended.

The ensuing searing pain inspired my vocal cords to discharge at decibel levels loud enough to rattle the windows. Certain that my finger had just burst into flame, I erupted into a forerunner of a break-dance. While holding my blistered digit at arm's length, I alternated between frantically jumping up and down and rolling around on the floor. Throughout the scintillating action, Grandpa remained as stoic as a monk. Finally, the pain subsided and my theatrics grew less dramatic. Then, without glancing up from his paper, Grandpa said, "SEE." His mentorship method may have been a tad dispassionate, but it worked. There was no denying, I did indeed see.

During the next summer, a similar illustration occurred when our family was camped at a lake. I discovered a small hole in the ground and began pouring dirt into it. My father warned that there were bees in that opening and if I didn't stop, I would get stung. In another instance of sluggish learning, I ignored his advice.

So excruciating was the consequent sting that I kicked off one of my shoes hard enough to send it sailing over my head. In the midst of performing a spectacle similar to the one in the kitchen, I glanced to see dear old Dad calmly going about his business. When the dust finally settled, chip off the old-school block that he was, Pop said, "SEE." Once again, I did clearly see.

Sadly, things didn't get much better as I grew older. For instance, I didn't catch on that climbing trees could be dangerous until the day I fell out of one. Having watched, Dad insightfully observed that the jolting re-acquaintance with the ground had stimulated a learning reflex deep within my cranium. Thus, by again ignoring the emotional turmoil of the moment, he led me to realize that my personal key to learning was pain. Logically, Pop advised my teachers that, if they wanted me to learn something, they should—"write it on a board and hit me over the head with it. "

So, for a while, to avoid the pain associated with learning, I purposefully put limited effort into my studies. As a result, during that time, I did well at the subjects that wouldn't earn me a dime in this world, and not so good at those subjects that would have led to a lucrative life.

Fortunately, in the end, I surmounted the well-intentioned efforts of my paternal counselors and graduated from high school. True to form, instead of a graduation present, Pop got me a "token of his astonishment." Even so, I'm pretty sure both Grandpa and Dad would have been proud if they'd lived to see the day I graduated from college. Still, without their old-school mentorship during my formative years, I might still be falling from trees.

Perfection Punctured

Recollections of a long-ago dilemma

This morning, just in time, I noticed a patch of ice on the cement stoop outside my door. That sobering sight reminded me of a February morning, during my junior high school days. In a shocking departure from the norm, I arrived at school early. While traversing the sidewalk leading to the school's entry doors, I slipped on some ice hidden under the snow. In a praiseworthy exhibition of agility, I executed a series of pioneering gymnastics before crash landing.

Like any normal adolescent boy, my first impulse was to assuage my dented pride. Clearly, assuagement would only be achieved by relishing the mortifying crash of the next hapless casualty. Hence, I positioned myself far enough behind the entry door windows to remain obscure, while still maintaining a splendid view of the sidewalk. I then waited for the unlucky nerd to show up. To my uneasiness, before long, a classmate appeared who was anything but a nerd.

Priscilla was a straight-A student. Rumor had it she had never dangled a participle, sung a sour note, fractured a fraction, or suffered a subject-verb disagreement. She was, quite simply, academic excellence personified. Hence, she'd been christened by her numerous intellectual inferiors as, "Priscilla Perfect." It's only natural to conclude such a person was the subject of mass loathing. However, there was one hindrance to collective abhorrence: Priscilla was also the prettiest girl in the 7th grade.

Focused on the warmth waiting inside the school, the dazzling damsel advanced at a crisp pace. As she drew near the icy patch, I faced the wrenching moral dilemma of whether or not to shout a warning. Then, just as I moved to warn her, a piercing shriek rang out. Instantly, the sound of that dented-pride-assuaging resonance trumped any amorous or humanitarian concerns I formerly harbored.

Gratified, I watched as the Flawless One's feet shot from under her. Her arms flew outward, flinging books in a nearly symmetrical arch. At the apex of Priscilla's ascent, a sizeable space separated the seat of her jeans from the sidewalk. The look of panic in her saucer-sized, baby-blues was soul-stirring. Upon impact, Priscilla's lips oscillated rapidly across her clenched pearly-whites.

With her perfection punctured, the wretched victim sat motionless while assorted papers floated down around her. Her peaches and cream complexion had turned to scarlet. In seconds, Miss Perfect was transformed from a vision of beauty to looking as though she'd spent the night in a dumpster.

After regaining her senses, Priscilla anxiously pivoted her head around to see if anyone had witnessed the unspeakable spectacle. When she noticed a set of widely grinning teeth inside the entry door windows, her mouth assumed a murderous scowl. At that point, I hastily retreated up the stairs and into the boy's restroom, where I hid until the school filled with students. Then, I entered the hallway, only to find myself nose-to-nose with a disheveled demon.

"IT WAS YOU, WASN'T IT?" The damning words flustered me. My strident requests for evidence, proving her accusation, were met with indifference. My protestations of innocence fell on deaf ears. Miss Perfect was convinced I was the despicable villain who had facilitated her disgrace. Before triumphantly departing, she showered me with terms slandering my mental stability. Even then, I had to admit, the girl looked gorgeous. Not long after, our family moved away. I never saw Priscilla again. To this day, I doubt she ever knew how smitten I was with her or how close I came to warning her on that long ago morning.

TECHNOLOGY-CHALLENGED

Uncontrolled Self-control

Some pros and cons regarding a new technology

Like many folks, the recent blizzard of technological innovation has left me feeling somewhat bewildered. No doubt the latest mobile devices do offer numerous practical applications. Still, as I see it, many other applications amount to little more than busy-work.

Then again, just last week, on the television news, I saw a preview of a mobile technology that truly caught my attention. As I watched in amazement, the newscaster declared that some automobile manufacturers were designing self-driving, "autonomous" automobiles. The screen then showed footage of functioning prototypes, already being tested. As detailed, a computerized combination of radar, cameras, ultrasonic sensors and laser scanners will "control" the steering wheel, brakes, horn, headlights, etc. Lastly, the anchorman stated that these wonder cars would be available soon.

At first glance, I was enthusiastic about this new concept. Here at last was a technology with real-world, practical purpose, in spades. Then suddenly, a disturbing scenario flashed through my mind. I imagined that, convinced by said technology the coast was clear, the first self-driving "autonomous" car passed another car in a blinding blizzard only to run headlong into the first "stealth" car, coming from the other direction.

With my cynicism duly restored, I began to evaluate these mega-tech autos more critically. Whereupon, I wondered what Tri-Cities-specific motoring situations the designers would fail to anticipate. For instance, what about the whitetail deer that hunker in the bushes along the Pony Road, waiting until a driver's nose hairs are countable before rocketing in front of an oncoming vehicle? As a direct result of these exhilarating occurrences, even our most experienced local drivers have pasted their lips to their windshields, at least once. Under such circumstances, it's hard to imagine a self-controlled, operating system that could detect the threat and stop quickly enough to prevent unsightly slobber marks.

Further, how about those patches of winter ice which develop only beneath the shadowed, northern corners on the east-west, running Cardwell Road? Will the new self-steering system be able to perform an adroit, 360-degree turn, and have the vehicle facing forward before it zips off the ice and back onto the dry pavement? Also, how will the autonomous-steering compensate when the infamous Norris Flat crosswind blows the automobile up on two wheels?

Still, if an accident does occur, the driver's (hereafter referred to as the passive-non-operator) hands will be free to cover his or her eyes, thus allowing for focused spiritual remorse. Less physical effort expended in steering means more energy retained for full-throated screaming. Also, because the wonder car was in command, there's no need to apologize to resentful passengers.

Even better, a passive-non-operator can look a disapproving, law-enforcement officer squarely in the eye and honestly proclaim, "I did not hit that police cruiser." Most notably, if neither passive-non-operator involved in a crash is driving their autonomous vehicles, lawyers won't know whom to sue.

As can be seen, self-driving, autonomous automobiles are a mixed blessing. So, before dashing out to purchase one, I believe I'll wait until all the kinks have been worked out. Paint me tentative, but I'd rather let some other adventurous soul (victim) discover what doesn't work as advertised. Eventually, I have little doubt that cars will not only drive themselves, but also trim the occupants' toenails, balance the checkbook and burp the baby. In the meantime, I think "speed control" is the only self-driving control I plan to relinquish—albeit only when appropriate.

Sneaky Snapping

Some thoughts on a privacy-depleting trend

Just the other day, while surfing the Internet, I saw a picture of a man who had fallen down a flight of stairs. He was sprawled across the lower end of the stairway. His briefcase had burst open, and papers were strewn about. The young man's clothing was in disarray. He didn't seem to be hurt, but he did look awfully embarrassed. Obviously, he didn't take the picture. Just as clearly, he wouldn't have wanted the picture taken. Yet, there, for the entire world to see was the image of his humiliating misfortune.

Like it or not, we have reached a time when many people carry mobile cameras (cell phone, iPhones, etc.) at all times. Things have gotten so bad it is wise to assume that, if one suffers an awkward mishap, someone will be present to photograph his or her not-so-shining moment. To my dismay, this privacy-depleting trend has become so popular that such photos have been dubbed "sneakies."

Still, to be fair, sneakies can be used constructively to modify behavior. For instance, in the Tri-city area, they have discouraged such unsavory practices as:

- Indiscreet scratching
- Family dumpster-diving
- Drinking from the milk carton
- Cleaning the dishes, once a week, using Mop & Glo
- Anonymously depositing unsolicited zucchini on neighbors' porches
- Parading around the house in the buff
- Retrieving the morning paper in one's long-johns and

snowshoes
- Dusting the living room with a leaf blower
- Eating spaghetti with the hands at the local cafe
- Road-kill/table-fare retrieval
- Winter time, ice-wind sailing on the main street

On the other hand, some unscrupulous sneakie-snappers have gleefully recorded such locally taboo, photographic subjects as:

- An image of a yawning resident that makes their driver's license picture look glamorous
- A hunter answering the call of nature in the deep woods behind Pony
- A fly fisherman slyly inserting a worm on his fly hook while trout fishing at Harrison lake
- An inattentive Norris Post Office patron repeatedly trying to open someone else's mailbox

After due deliberation, I believe Tri-cities' sneakies have the potential to do more harm than good. In addition to having raised area tension levels, they are also objectionable for the following reasons:

- The innocent yokel may never know that he or she is a sneakie-star, until it's too late.
- Further, the victim may never know who the sneaky perpetrator was that took the sneakie.
- Even worse, there is a chance the sneakie could be posted on the Internet.
- Whereupon said sneakie will have progressed to become a viral "peekie."
- Most deplorably, the local bumpkin will have won global acclaim of the sort he or she never desired.

Consequently, given the current dearth of privacy, it

would make sense to close all the curtains and hunker in my house. However, that's not my definition of living. So, I reckon I'll just go on being me and doing what I do. Then if a local phone-photo-fan wants to snap a sneakie of me and post it as a peekie, have at it. However, peek at your own risk. I'm too old and jaded to be easily embarrassed.

Texting Divided

Some thoughts concerning out-of-the-lane electronic messaging

Not long ago, I saw on the Internet where an American college has divided some of their stairway steps into three separate lanes: 1) walking, 2) running, and 3) texting. As per school officials, the painted lines are not intended to direct traffic flow. Rather the project is meant to be a lighthearted way to draw students' attention to the problem of distracted people walking into one another.

At any rate, in the photograph accompanying the article, the stairway appears to be of standard width. No signs specify one-way traffic. So, one is left to assume foot traffic can both ascend and descend said stairs in all three tracks simultaneously. Most significantly, the running lane is positioned in the middle of the stairs—adjacent to the texting lane.

Under such circumstances, one doesn't need a doctorate in human behavior to foresee that, despite the project's lighthearted intent, the results will likely be anything but amusing. Although not intended to direct traffic flow, undoubtedly, some non-texting runners will utilize those divided tracks to enlighten inconsiderate texters to the error of their ways. Sooner or later, a disgruntled runner, descending the stairs, will notice a dawdling, distracted texter ascending ahead. Seeing a long-awaited chance to avenge for countless previous screeching halts and slopped lattes, he or she then "accidentally" swerves across the lane and bashes into the texter at full throttle.

In the process, the cell phone gets jarred loose and bounces down the stairs, into the runner's track, where it instantly transforms into a high-tech banana peel. The avenging stair sprinter then slips on it, does an airborne cartwheel, and lands in the midst of a bunch of innocent walkers. One shudders to envision the bout of triple-lane stair rage sure to ensue. Needless to say, between the initial collision, the pileup, and the rage, the chances of severe injury will be high.

Worse yet, if this experiment becomes the norm nationwide, the multitude of similar violent encounters sure to follow would necessitate the development of such new medical terminology as:

- phone-to-bone compound fracture
- smashed smartphone stupor syndrome
- distraction-actuated denture dislocation
- Blackberry buttock bruise
- texting thumb thrombosis
- keypad-cranium collision concussion—and
- wireless word processor puncture wound

In summation, despite their project's faults, the school's administrators are to be applauded for their out-of-the-lane thinking. Furthermore, what better place to perform such a complex experiment than an institution of higher learning? In that way, a lengthy study of the project can be conducted, and the results published as a public service warning entitled, "News Flash! Texters aren't always aware of where they're going."

Seriously texter dudes! When I was in school, students weren't nearly as technologically sophisticated as they are today. However, unlike a herd of lemmings, we did know better than to launch successive breakable bodies over a gaping stairwell without first looking where to place our feet. What can be so monumentally important that it needs to be addressed while utilizing stairs? I thought the whole idea of attending college was to get smart.

Dimensionally Driven

Some novel suggestions for a new technology

This week, I have been hearing a lot about yet another stunning technological development—the 3D printer. As I understand it, a 3D printer can produce a three-dimensional solid object from a digital model using such materials as steel, ceramics, sterling silver, sandstone, brass, rubber, bronze, and plastic. Such a wide variety of materials allows for creating such useful products as back scratchers, coat hooks, doorknobs, bikinis, and shoes. Further, 3D printers may soon be capable of printing food, including meat and chocolate. Perhaps most exciting, certain big box stores are currently in the process of setting up, on-site, 3D Printing Stations. Thus, before long, customers will be able to bring their 3D-ready, digital files and generate their customized items right in the store. With my curiosity duly sparked, I began imagining personal applications for this wondrous new technology.

To begin, I envisioned myself standing in a big box store, watching my cavernous, pie-hole conforming, slobber-resistant, ceramic coffee mug being fashioned before my incredulous eyes. Then, I perceived supping my morning coffee from said mug, as my nose-wart and hearing aid frame-accommodating, plastic reading glasses were crafted. Lastly, I visualized using said spectacles to read the morning paper while my bite-pattern-proportioned, blueberry breakfast bagel was being fashioned.

With my fertile mind now fully engaged, a multitude of other 3D printer adaptations fairly burst forth. For instance, a jilted teenage girl could throw a party for her girlfriends that featured a printed, 3D chocolate mold of her ex-boyfriend's head and shoulders. Said artistic confection then could serve as a conversation piece, an object of collective loathing, and a taste-bud-titillating dessert. Even better, as the evening's crowning event, a drawing could be held to determine which lucky guest gets to hack off the honoree's deceiving lips.

On the family front, parents can soon record their kids' annual growth with ceramic, 3D skull molds, complete with acne, tattoos, nose rings, spiked hair, etc. Thus, unlike traditional door jamb marks, this new method would record both physical development and psychological development/ regression. Additionally, come autumn, parents could use them as Halloween decorations.

Those interested in archeology might use 3D printers for replicating such priceless family artifacts as great-great grandpa's brass chamber pot. People who value their privacy might want to consider creating a rubber door knocker in the form of their clenched fist with attached brass knuckles facing outward. Gardeners could digitally record themselves immediately upon rising from bed, before grooming, and print out a full-body, sandstone replication. Said horrifying device could then serve as a sure-fire scarecrow, capable of warding off the most brazen of starving men, beasts, and bugs. So far as concerns bikinis, I am pretty sure there aren't yet any 3D micro-printers small enough to print the current skimpy versions.

Most astonishing, bio-3D printers are capable of printing replicated human organs. Hence, I envision surgical patients being able to succumb to anesthetic-induced slumber while listening to the reassuring sounds of their new spleen being fashioned nearby. Thus, the malfunctioning organ can be carved out and tossed into the trash can while, at the same moment, the 3D wonder-device burps out the shiny new spleen which will be forthrightly slapped into place. Hence, both time and money are saved.

As can be seen, 3d printing may well revolutionize the way people live. Its potential applications are almost limitless. Who knows, someday it may even be possible to print out a 3D model of a 3D character from a 3D movie. Now that would be something to see.

Hack Attack

Reflections on robbery, then and now

There have been thieves for as long as there have been valuables. However, over time, much has changed in the way robbery is carried out. For instance, not long ago, my email account was hacked. To make a long story short, I ended up having to cancel credit cards and get new ones. I also had to cancel the payments on several bills I hadn't charged. Since that hack attack, my enthusiasm for computer communications has dimmed considerably. In fact, nowadays, whenever I send an e-mail message, it feels as though I'm sending my digital jugular vein across cyberspace for legions of high-tech crooks to take a hack at.

All in all, it's enough to make a guy long for the Old West days. Back then, unlike today's shadowy thieves, a road agent at least had the strength of character to rob a man face-to-face. Sure, he wore a mask, but at any rate, he did make eye contact with his prey. Further, it required a measure of physical labor to carry off the pilfered gold and silver coins. By contrast, in his attempt to rob me, an anonymous hacker effortlessly slithered a cursor across a computer monitor screen to access my email address, decipher my password, and steal my personal data.

As a rule, a road agent seldom felt obliged to leave a mail address at which he could be contacted later. Further, he just didn't have time to dilly-dally around with tricky passwords. Rather, to gain access to another's valuables, the rough and ready lawbreaker's password was apt to be short and easy-to-understand, like "Stick em up!"

Then again, because the outlaw's version of a password

was issued audibly, there was always a chance the victim might identify his voice. What's more, because the robber used a horse to beat a getaway, the robbed individual might recognize the horse. Thus, the fiscally injured party would have had the option of paying a visit to the outlaw's hideaway and robbing him back. In comparison, the modern hacker can steal personal information from the far-flung corners of the earth. Then he can use that data to empty the hackee's checking account with scant fear of ever being identified. Still, a hacker doesn't pose a direct threat to one's physical well being.

Indeed, it is an undeniable fact that the road agent often brandished a firearm in order to encourage compliance. Consequently, a hesitant target ran a high risk of getting shot dead. But then, a captured highway man was regularly subjected to terminal justice at the hands of territorial vigilantes, thereby providing a degree of moral victory to the deceased victim. So, despite the harrowing circumstances, one can understand how a surviving victim might grant such a daring desperado a grudging level of respect.

All things considered, as I see it, being boldly robbed up close and personal by a road agent, was just plain more sporting than being swindled by a faceless techno-geek from a hidden location. I was lucky not to have suffered a significant financial loss. As a result, I live for the day when technology provides me a chance to launch a hack-back-hack-attack on the cowardly perpetrator of my recent hack attack. I won't rest easy until, like the fleas of a thousand camels, my Internet viruses and malware have infested every last one of his computer files. Then maybe he'll long for the days of old too.

Harrison, Montana
The Town Haul Cafe: Social Mecca of the Tri-cities

Random Ruminations

True-Blue Son of the Northland

Reflections on a half frozen life, fully savored

The die was cast early. I was born in the month of January during a howling blizzard. According to my dad, I entered this world as pure as the driven snow and with a face as blue as lake ice. My initial inhalation culminated with a sneeze in the doctor's face. Dad swore that, with my second exhalation, he could see my breath. Unlike most newborns, instead of crying and fussing, I coughed and hacked. My nose began to run even before my eyes opened. Perhaps most telling of all, (again, according to Dad) my first purposeful deed was to fart—due north. In sum, I entered this world as a "true-blue son of the northland."

At home, each morning, Mother defrosted my diapers in the oven, next to the breakfast rolls. Vaguely, I recall shoveling snow from my playpen with a Captain America toy shield. While still a toddler, I froze my butt to an ice cold potty training seat. While being pried from the seat's cruel grip, I instinctively began yodeling. To further toughen me up, Dad insisted that my birthday cakes be made of ice cream. It worked. By the time I was five, I was eating snow and discharging ice cubes.

With toughening came enlightenment in matters vital to northland survival. For instance, I soon learned that an icicle, after falling on one's head, produces a rising lump. My early mastery of mature words began when I slipped on some ice and fell down the church steps after Sunday school. My first physical altercation was a snowball fight, from which I learned how to stand up for myself while ducking behind a parked car. Emboldened, I next discovered how to reduce the most belligerent of bullies to a sniveling pacifist with the mere flick of a finger to the back of his frostbitten ear.

Further illumination ensued as I grew older. I recognized that when crossing ice, immersed in melt water, one can slip, fall and land so rapidly as to render the mind incapable of keeping up with events. On the other hand, slipping on snow-buried lumber showed me that it is possible to consciously execute a flying, reverse somersault from the tuck position before gravity is able to take effect. I also found out that, despite the real possibility of snow blindness, it's always better to keep one's eyes open when skiing downhill. These and countless other revelations have allowed me to not only survive, but to thrive in this place I was born to love.

So, as for me, I'll continue to choose to live in the northland, nestled in the midst of the mountains. After all, if the leaves never fall from the trees, one misses the magic of seeing them grow back. If winter doesn't come, folks don't get to experience the snug splendor of a white Christmas. And if the flowers bloom the year round, people will never stand in a mountain meadow in June, with snow still around its edges, and savor the sight of glacier lilies.

In the end, it seems to add a peaceful continuity to my life, watching the seasons come and go and awaiting the next. And that's why I'll exit this world as I entered it—as a true-blue son of the northland. After which, I'll be laid beneath its hallowed soil. That's if the ground isn't frozen rock solid.

Potty Prose

A few literacy-enhancing suggestions

Recently, at the school where I am employed, we have experienced a veritable burgeoning of student writing. Not your ordinary, everyday classroom writing exercises mind you, but rather those pearls of wisdom one sees scribbled on restroom walls. Goodness knows, I am for human artistic expression in all its various forms. However, I must admit, I am appalled by the shocking lack of creative pride demonstrated in our contemporary potty prose. In truth, many of the phrases I have observed could be seen, word-for-word, on bathroom walls when I was a youngster. Further, I have little doubt that some of these same treasured axioms were secretively chiseled, millennia ago, in Latin, on the walls of ancient Roman baths. In short, many of the literary classics blossoming across our school's restroom walls are examples of plagiarism at its worst. Furthermore, I seriously doubt that our modern stall scrawlers even know the definition of "plagiarism" let alone the seriousness of the offense.

Always on the lookout for educational opportunities, it struck me that possibly we could use our current epidemic of potty prose as a way to increase learning. To begin, I suggest that the school require all restroom free-lancers to cite the sources of their writing in a bibliography. The bibliography would be written directly below the quote on the stall, using proper Modern Language Association (MLA) citation format. Authors would be listed alphabetically by their last names, book titles underlined, publisher's name and location listed, plus the date of publication—all of course correctly indented, punctuated, and spaced.

Every quote and citation would be reviewed, on location, by the English department and graded accordingly as part of the writer's semester English grade. Those lavatory journalists who brazenly ignored the requirements would suffer a failing semester grade for the unforgivable literary felony of plagiarism. Those with the creative genius to write new, previously unpublished potty prose would, of course, simply list themselves as the author in the citation.

Enacting these simple academic requirements could greatly reduce the number of amateurs writing on our bathroom walls and, at the same time, encourage linguistic excellence among the truly talented in our midst. Additionally, the offshoot of this modest exercise could lead to a plethora of new learning opportunities. The sky's the limit, folks.

Why, we could sponsor a bathroom wall-writing contest, with the winning prose (and the stall that it is written on) displayed on the steps of the state capitol. Picture if you can, the proud parents standing beside their beaming child, clutching his or her cherished stall as the news cameras roll. Even better, with a little effort, we could move the ignoble art of potty prose from the covert to the celebrated and, at the same time, put our little town on the map. Food for thought, eh?

Less-than-shining Moments

Recalling a few mega-mortifying mishaps

Overall, despite life's many adversities, I have managed to conduct myself in this world with a reasonable degree of decorum. Regrettably, I have also endured some, what can best be described as "less-than-shining moments." Without doubt, the most mortifying example occurred some years ago during a civil trial for which I had been selected to serve on the jury. Unfortunately, before the proceedings even began, the seeds of calamity were already in place.

To begin, the outside temperature was twenty degrees below zero while the courtroom felt like a sauna. In addition, as is common knowledge, civil trials are notoriously boring. Moreover, spring-mounted chairs allowed for jurors to, periodically, shift their body positions, thereby enhancing comfort levels. Lastly, to make matter worse, I chose a seat in the back row of the jury box.

As the proceedings dragged on, the combination of stupor-inducing heat, boring dialogue, and a too-comfortable chair, began to take their toll. My eyelids grew heavy, and I relaxed more and more into my flexible chair. Then, I succumbed to sweet slumber.

"Whap"—the sound of my head bashing against the wall behind the jury box resonated throughout the courtroom. In a flash, I recoiled back to an upright position, fully awake. A deafening silence ensued, during which every eye in the courtroom, including the judge's, was riveted on my radish-hued face.

Not knowing what else to do, I flashed my warmest smile and waved to let everyone know I was okay. Judging by his protracted, scathing stare, I don't believe His Honor was overly concerned about my well being. After what seemed an eternity, the trial resumed. From then on, I remained zealously attentive. Not surprisingly, since that less-than-shining moment, I have never again been asked to serve on a jury.

Another mega-mortifying mishap occurred at a drivers' license renewal station. For the preceding four days, I had been working long hours. As a result, I was even less mentally acute than normally. Nevertheless, I was intent on getting the odious task out of the way. So, I arrived just as the station opened. Groggy though I was, I managed to complete the required paperwork and pass the eye exam.

At that time, the uniformed Department of Transportation employee told me to place my toes on a blue line, painted on the floor. After focusing on getting my toes perfectly flush to the line, I lifted my head and found myself staring at a wall. Immediately, a voice, dripping with sarcasm, proclaimed, "Sir, would you mind turning around? We need a picture of your face, not the back of your head."

Naturally, the last thing on earth I wanted to do was to grant that smart butt the satisfaction of turning around. In fact, for a few seconds, I seriously considered shimmying across the room and out the door backwards. However, because the paperwork was already partially completed, I had no choice but to comply with the degrading request.

To this day, I can still see the foul smirk on her face as the Wicked Witch of Wretched Portrayals concluded the licensing process. Granted, driver's license photos are infamously hideous, but that one turned out to be the worst such picture I ever had taken. I looked like an alpha-male gorilla with rabies.

Ultimately, the above-described events were not the only less-than-shining moments I have suffered. They do, however, still rank as my most mega-mortifying examples. Here's hoping they remain so.

Got the Cheap Gas

The pros and cons of lower fuel prices

Not long ago, I stopped at a gas station to fuel up. As luck would have it, that very morning, the price per gallon of regular-grade gasoline had fallen below two dollars. When I first noticed the monumental adjustment, I was flabbergasted. However, it didn't take me long to recover. Without forethought, I quickly found myself mimicking the victory dance of the guy who wins the cold cuts on a current TV commercial. At the same time, like the cold cut winner, I repeatedly chanted, "Got the cheap gas. Got the cheap gas. Woo!"

When, at last, I nervously looked around, it was apparent that the other patrons shared my bliss. Rather than being frowned upon or derided, I was greeted with unrestrained smiles and shouts of encouragement. The communal exuberance was such that complete strangers exchanged congratulatory back thumps. One fellow was so beside himself that he just stood in place and jumped up and down.

Although I'm sure it took the same amount of time as usual to fill my tank, not having to watch bankruptcy-generating numbers add up made it seem a lot faster. When finished, to my immense satisfaction, I had enough money left over to buy a cup of coffee to go. Thanks to bent fracking, I was no longer cents lacking.

On the road again, it occurred to me that, because gas prices had gone down, the price of other petroleum-based products must inevitably follow. Hence, my future monthly credit card statements would be even less traumatizing. With dollar signs dancing in my head, I put the pedal to the metal and hurried home to Internet research those bank-account-enlarging oil byproducts. To say the list was lengthy would be an understatement.

Initially, I was surprised to discover that neither coffee nor chewing tobacco is a petroleum-based product. Nevertheless, many of the goods I did find listed were of the category one would expect to see. I refer to such seemingly appropriate items as automobile tires, asphalt shingles, antifreeze, fertilizer, bearing grease, and shoe polish. Additionally, I was pleased to find that the list of oil-derivative products included those cherished all-American favorites: footballs, basketballs, and golf balls.

On the other hand, I was troubled by the number of seemingly inappropriate items included in the list. In particular, I refer to those petroleum-based goods meant to be smeared on human skin, like soap and deodorant. Even more unsavory were such cherished feminine grooming staples as perfume and (believe it or not) lipstick.

Most shocking was the number of fuel-derivative products I discovered that were intended for use inside the human body. In particular, I refer to such merchandise as toothbrushes, toothpaste, dentures, denture adhesive, food preservatives, aspirin, and even artificial heart valves.

Not to be oversensitive, but I found the thought of brushing my pearly whites with a paste derived from a licorice-hued, gooey fossil fuel to be quite disturbing. Even more alarming was the possibility that my heart might someday be dependent on an artificial valve partially comprised of a slimy substance that had been sucked from the earth's bowels.

Obviously, the advantages of lower fuel prices turned out to be a mixed bag. However, the big bucks I stood to save eventually overcame any qualms I had about using petroleum-based products—or, to put it more succinctly: "Got the cheap gas. Got the cheap gas. Woo!"

Resuscitation Revised

Some revolutionary thoughts on a life-saving procedure

For a long time, every two years, I have been updating my coronary, pulmonary resuscitation (CPR) skills. Each time, it's the same thing: opening the airway, chest compressions, rescue breaths, etc. Sure, CPR-masks are available for professional emergency personnel. However, for the impromptu aid-giver, such masks are seldom available. Hence, if called on to give rescue breaths, I would be required to engage in mouth-to-mouth contact with complete strangers. Like many folks, the social awkwardness of such an act makes me uncomfortable with rescue breaths.

Obviously, the situation cries out for a new system. At such times, all it takes is for one bold, free-thinker to look at the problem from a new perspective. Thus, after a period of deliberation, the idea hit me like a thunderclap: Why not give CPR with a sink plunger?

Indeed, the idea is so simple and obvious, it's a marvel no one has thought of it before. With the current method, precious time is spent tilting the head, depressing the tongue, pinching the nose, and extending the jaw. By contrast, with my innovative technique, the CPR-practitioner simply flops the cupped, rubber plunger over the nose and mouth (thereby forming the all-important seal) and immediately begins propelling life-saving air into sagging lungs. Meanwhile, his or her teammate would jump-start the heart with chest compressions. Like a finely-oiled machine, a well-trained duo of chugger and compressor could substantially increase cardio-pulmonary-resuscitation efficiency. Even better, the chance of personal-contact-disease-transmission, so common with traditional CPR, is all but eliminated.

Additionally, conscious patients will see at a glance that help is at hand. A note of caution though: often such patients, deliriously grateful for their deliverance, may start flailing their arms and hands wildly. At the mere sight of a determined rescuer dashing to their aid, plunger at the ready, their emotions might simply overwhelm them—so much so that, to the untrained eye, it may seem that victims are intentionally trying to beat the instrument of their resuscitation away. Fortunately, trained aid-givers will recognize the situation for what it is and, oblivious to hysterics, press on with their mission of propelling compassion.

As well, the rhythmic "chugga-chugga-chugga" "thump-thump-thump" of trained CPR volunteers at work will serve as a soothing solace, assuring concerned bystanders that the patient is receiving the best modern medicine has to offer. Even better, the humble heroes will earn the undying gratitude of the resuscitated (although the more timid may decline to express their feelings until after the plunger ring has dissipated).

Of course, I cannot stress strongly enough that every effort must be made to ensure that sink plungers used for CPR are used solely for that purpose. It is imperative that each one be clearly labeled: "Pulmonary Plunger - For Use On Stopped Lungs Only" Most crucially, never—never, under any circumstances, use a flange (toilet) plunger for CPR.

Frankly, I suspect overcoming the public's unsavory perception of plungers in general will be the greatest obstacle facing pulmonary plungers. Further, the medical profession does not abandon established procedure impulsively. Hence, despite its tantalizing potential, current CPR methods will doubtless remain in effect until after my revised resuscitation technique has been exhaustively tested. Even then, broad approval is not a given. I'll keep ya posted.

Say What?

Dealing with hearing impairment

My first memorable event with the audibly challenged took place when I was eleven years-old. Because I had a newspaper route at the time, ornery canines were a fact of life. Therefore, I thought it wise to purchase a newly touted whistle that sounded at a decibel level that, while not discernable to humans, was intolerable to dogs. The next morning, sure enough, a fanged Fido came racing toward me while growling menacingly. While blowing my wonder whistle with eyeball-bulging effort, I watched incredulously as the obviously deaf flea bag bit my ankle. I retreated with my foolproof bite preventer still clamped in my teeth. While I couldn't imagine it at the moment, that dog's impairment was to play a major role in my own life later.

Some years afterward, the Army's legendary love affair with thunderous explosives, caused me to develop a condition known as "tinnitus." Simply put, tinnitus is a perpetual, loud ringing in the ears. Obviously, individuals such as me struggle to comprehend much of what is going on around them. Regrettably, this conspicuous condition is often misconstrued as dimwittedness.

Additionally, folks blessed with normal hearing often assume sound-hindered folks experience a comparatively more tranquil internal environment. On the contrary, for those enduring tinnitus, the din inside their heads never ceases. Of course, my choices of succeeding civilian employment as a meat cutter, carpenter, and heavy-equipment operator only increased the shrill chaos within my skull.

As a result, I have been a card-carrying member of the "Say what? Society" for over forty years. After that many years, the phrase has become my automatic response to most of what is said. So much so that some folks that have known me for an extended time habitually repeat every sentence to avoid the inevitable, "Say what?"

Over the years, my lack of sound perception prowess has resulted in some noteworthy experiences. One example occurred while I was working at a mine as a foreman overseeing heavy equipment operators. After having endured more "say what's" than any mortals deserved, my crew offered to buy me a "hearing-ear-dog." Whenever danger lurked that I was unable to hear, as a warning, this uniquely trained male canine was to lift his leg on me. Adroitly seeing through this backhanded benevolence, I replied that their "generosity was exceeded only by their enormously perverted minds."

Finally, after receiving threats of physical maltreatment, I invited a salesman to demonstrate a hearing aid at my house. After tinkering with it for a few minutes, he inserted the device into my left ear. By that time, I had need of the bathroom. Upon flushing the commode, I nearly jumped through the bathroom window. To my previously naive hearing orifices, the raucous roar sounded as though a grenade had just exploded beneath my backside. Clearly, I had forgotten why a toilet is often referred to as a "thunder mug." Not overly impressed, I asked the salesman the price of the device. His response of "$1,250.00 per ear" convinced me that it would be more fiscally prudent to have folks repeat themselves.

Actually, I consider that I hear tolerably well so long as there is no significant background noise, such as a house fly stomping across the ceiling. Further, I honestly believe that if my central-cranial clamor were ever to cease, I would be reduced to a piteous, blithering wretch within minutes.

On the contrary, there are certain advantages to being audibly challenged. For instance, I am no longer invited to go rattlesnake hunting. When told that my trousers are unzipped, because I would have no idea what was said, there is no cause for indignity. Instead, accompanied by a cordial smile, my most likely reply would be, "How nice."

Similarly, imagine how boring conversation would be without people like me. Rather than sitting there like a group of whispering bores, the sound-discernment-deprived add the drama of ear cartilage cupping, shouting, extremity-flailing animation and spirited efforts at drawing pictures in the air. Just try having a private conversation in a public place with a "say-what" afflicted person. Then, consider the strangers who would otherwise be deprived of the juicy tidbits of said "confidential" exchange.

Finally, in a "ringing'" endorsement of "say what" sufferers everywhere, I even forgave that ill-tempered dog of my youth Grudgingly, I had to admit that if I had been confronted by a scarlet-faced, swollen-cheeked, onion-eyed life-form, silently stalking toward my house, I might have mauled the ominous looking alien myself.

Starter Fluid

Some deliberations on the morning tonic

Sometimes waking up is like slogging through an impenetrable fog. This morning was such an occasion. Feeling like a mummy's curse, I staggered from the bedroom. Then, with barely attuned senses, I stalked the beckoning fragrance emanating from my preset percolator. Upon arriving at the hallowed destination, I mechanically poured a cup of "starter fluid."

As the first swallow splashed into an empty stomach, my mind grudgingly stirred to primitive perception, which led to such existential inquiries as: "Where the blazes am I? Am I still in this world? How did I get here? Why am I here? Who am I? What am I? To whom am I posing these questions?"

By mid-cup, my eyes began to focus, which resulted in slightly more complex contemplation such as: "What's up with that luminosity coming through the windows? What day is it? Whose hand is holding that mug of what looks like mud? and, If this is consciousness, I don't like it."

Thus did the laborious process continue until, at the last slurp from the initial cupful, I felt the first discernible heart beat of the day. Upon achieving that reassuring milestone, it was time for a second cup. It was also time for work.

These days, work consists of writing, or as I prefer to think of it, "recording my blather." Clasping the warm coffee mug in both hands while the computer loaded, I unlimbered my fingers enough to permit rudimentary typing. By midway through the second cup, I was whipping out 10-words-per-minute with no more than 10 mistakes. At the cup's final sip, my fingers were blazing across the key board at 45-words-per-minute and mostly hitting the right keys. Having reached my high-water typing rate, any lingering stupor was in full retreat. Even better, the words began to make sense.

As usual, by 9 am, my creativity spurt stalled. However, by then, I was also cordial enough to rejoin the human tribe. So, leaving the written word behind, I went to Harrison's cafe for an exercise in the spoken word and—more starter fluid. Soon, I was engaged in discussion by reliably opinionated locals, who gather at the restaurant daily. As usual, the conversations extended from "civil dialogue" to "vocal mayhem." While engaged in said exercise, the ebony elixir's effects continued to buoy my efforts by lubricating the vocal cords and loosening my tongue. Subsequently, my lips were stimulated to such feverish motion, that even a semi-introvert such as me was transformed to a commanding presence (aka boisterous motor mouth). Of course, my cohorts, equally buttressed with coffee, gruffly shouted over my pontifications, and I returned the favor. Thus did the linguistic parry and thrust continue until, with my starter fluid tolerance maxed-out, I virtually vibrated from the restaurant to complete the rest of my daily tasks.

In the final analysis, showing up for any activity before noon, without a coffee mug in hand, instantly brands one a slacker, not sufficiently wired for exertion. So, it should come as no surprise if some folks take affront to my seemingly ignoble term for their esteemed morning tonic. Nonetheless, I firmly maintain that it provides a more candid description than "coffee." Fact is, on mornings like today, my "starter fluid" literally ratchets the sun up from beneath the eastern horizon. Without it, I might not escape the fog of sleep to reach full awareness all day. Then again, there are other days when that might not be such a bad thing.

Lefty

Living in a hand-biased world

My father was left-handed. For some reason, he wanted a like-handed son. According to family lore, when I was still very young, Dad tied a barbecued pork chop to a string and lowered it into my crib. When my wee, south paw reached to seize the mesmerizing delicacy, he could barely contain his glee.

Initially, being opposite-handed from most of the world wasn't a big deal. However, upon reaching school age, I discovered that, fair or not, this world is designed for the right-handed. For instance, during the time period I attended middle school, fast drying ink had not yet been perfected. Like any student, I wrote from the left side of a paper to the right. So, my southpaw drug over whatever I had just written. Upon reaching the bottom of a page, my left hand emerged soiled with ink. Even worse, my teachers complained bitterly about my illegible work. While walking home from school, the sight of my ebony appendage caused passersby to gasp in horror at what they thought was gangrene. As a result, I was relegated to using previously-chewed, lead pencils while the "normal" students used shiny, new ink pens. Thus was the stage set for even greater indignities.

Beyond doubt, the most flagrant discrimination occurred during my military experience. Not to suggest they ever actually liked anyone, but Army drill sergeants held a special loathing for left-handed recruits. The brutal truth is, they considered "directionally disadvantaged" troops like me to be a curse on their profession. Sometimes it seemed my every movement drove them to fury. Little doubt my hearing loss began when crazed drill instructors piercingly declared the satanic roots of left-handedness, just inches from my ears.

Later, I worked as a carpenter in the Harrison area. At last, I had found redemption in that southpaws could work in situations difficult for a right-hander. Still, all was not harmony. Often, "standard-pawed" carpenters were brought to grief upon hearing that they would be unloading building materials with me. They were keenly aware that whenever two, hand-opposed carpenters carried sheet rock together, the accompanying, back-wrenching tussle often sent both to the chiropractor. About that time, mostly as an alarm to unsuspecting local tradesmen, I was nicknamed, "Lefty."

Another blatant slight involved the design of lock buttons for electric drills. Intended for drilling in continuous operation, said button was deliberately positioned where Lefty couldn't help but lock it on. Thus drill handles were routinely wrenched from my grip and, in propeller-like action, repeatedly whacked across my pearly whites. At times, it was impossible not to take personal offense.

Given all the above, the question begs, "Why would my father want a left-handed son?" Upon reflection, I reached the most plausible answer. Despite the indignities suffered, by virtue of my inherited contrary alignment, I have made this a more stimulating world. Like Pop, over the years, I annoyed, aggravated, exasperated, and drove to distress countless deserving right-handers—without even trying. Sadly, many still refuse to concede how boring their lives would have been without "Lefty."

The Golf Burger

An **exercise in convenient rationalization**

Several years ago, I read a magazine article extolling the virtues of a man who came up with the idea of putting advertisements in the bottoms of golf holes. So, he secured financial agreements between golf course owners and business advertisers to do just that. In exchange, the man received a share of the advertising revenues as his profit. Hence, when golfers retrieved their golf balls from said holes, they would be zapped with marketing to buy a burger or many other products. According to the article, this fellow was a poster person for free enterprise.

Personally, I thought the scoundrel should have been stoned off of every golf club in the land. After all, most golfers hit the links to get away from the pressures of the mercantile world. Further, in a sport where success depends on the ability to focus, I reckoned the last thing a golfer needed was to be distracted at every hole. Nevertheless, this wannabe tycoon devised a way to hound them from one end of the course to the other. The question begged—"Where will it end?"

With that question in mind, I began to imagine the logical evolution of such a process. As I saw it, it wouldn't be long before a customer went into a restaurant and ordered a cup of espresso and a bowl of five-alarm chili. Upon draining the espresso cup of its high-tension contents, the old boy noticed an ad for high-voltage, portable heart-defibrillators in the cup's bottom. Then, after scooping the last scalding spoonful of chili from the bottom of the bowl, he discovered an ad for EPA-approved, anti-ozone-killer breath mints.

Finally, before leaving said eatery, I envisioned the old boy deciding to use the restroom. Where, upon lifting the toilet lid, the astonished patron spied an advertisement in the bottom of the commode, urging him to check out the nearby Swirling Waters Spas and Hot Tubs retail store.

It was at that moment, I realized that, in my earnest desire to condemn commercialism gone amuck, I had inadvertently stumbled onto a surefire path to fame and riches for myself. All I needed to do was follow the lead of the afore-badmouthed golf burger entrepreneur and collect my share of commode advertising revenues. Talk about a captive audience. Why, in no time at all, I'd be renowned as the "Thunder Mug Mogul." People would point and say, "That guy made his fortune in marine-latrine marketing." From bath tissue to riches, it's the American way.

Regrettably, that would have required me to disavow my previously stated opposition to just such tactless commercialism. Then again, to be fair to myself, it took a person of uncommon entrepreneurial vision to recognize the money-making potential in potty product promotion. My dilemma was apparent. What to do?

Finally, I concluded that, no matter how unscrupulous the advertisements were, so long as they were located on private property, all was legal. And goodness knows I have great respect for the law. If I dare to say so myself, my clever resolution of the predicament represents convenient rationalization at its best. Oddly enough, to this day, I have failed to find financial backers to fund my surefire idea. Only time will tell how things go. In the meantime, I'm considering taking up golfing.

A Bleak Black Friday

An example of shopping at its most perilous

As I write, Thanksgiving is over, and Christmas is not far off. The holiday season began as well as could be expected. For instance, I am grateful that, after Thanksgiving dinner, I was more stuffed than had been the turkey. Additionally, following my post-feast power-nap, I took the time to give thanks for my many blessings.

Regrettably, my holiday spirit soon nose-dived when, on Thanksgiving evening, I turned the TV on to watch the evening news. One of the news reports focused on a mall security camera's recording of two women Christmas shopping. Both shoppers decided they absolutely had to have the same gift item—of which only one was left. In a flash, the situation degenerated to a rousing physical altercation. As candy-cane-clutching children looked on in horror, fists flew, hair was uprooted and language wholly unbecoming of the season drowned out pleas for civility.

Next, one of the Ultimate Fighting Championship wannabes scored a bone-crushing take down. A soul-stirring ground and pound session followed as the nattily-dressed "ladies" writhed about on the litter-strewn floor. Then, in a stunning finale, the gladiator who seemed to be getting the worst of it, unleashed a stun gun on her adversary.

Really! People actually pack concealed stun guns when shopping. What's next, bear spray and nun chucks? When did Christmas shopping become a form of martial arts? The report ended without revealing who got the treasured item. It would be fitting if an anonymous person took it while the two combatants were busy trying to tear each other limb-from-limb. Most sobering, the sorry spectacle took place before "Black Friday."

Come Black Friday (the day-after Thanksgiving), yet again, I gaped at the TV screen in disbelief as big box store employees were nearly trampled by frenzied mobs intent on getting the best bargains. To the uninitiated, the scene must have looked like a soccer riot. Like a human tsunami, the surging horde nearly destroyed a display of the newest electronic devices. Many men behaved as though they had gorged on performance enhancing steroids. None of the fellows, however, could match the vehemence demonstrated by some members of the gentler gender. In short, I've watched football games in which NFL linemen conducted themselves with more decorum. Initially, I was offended that the inaugural date for the Christmas shopping season had been dubbed with a name traditionally associated with a catastrophe. However, after observing the above-described exhibitions, I could no longer deny the term's validity.

After turning off the TV, I reflected on what I had seen over the previous two days. I concluded that, there was no product I desired so badly as to engage in kicking and gouging on a mall floor to obtain it. Hence, instead of going Christmas shopping at the mall, I am considering online shopping. Hopefully, that way I can avoid the intolerable indignity of being stun-gunned.

Ultimately, next year, I think the best gift we can all give to each other is to ignore Black Friday altogether. And instead, use that time to focus on the true intent of Thanksgiving and Christmas. Who knows, some folks might even be inspired to grow up.

Seasonal Bugs

Some candid observations concerning summer and winter bugs

After a summer of enduring countless attacks from summer bugs, winter's bugs have descended on me with a fury. Recently, I awoke with a nose that mimicked a leaky faucet, a throat that felt like I'd gargled with Drano, and a cough that seemed to originate from the marrow in my toe bones. Advancing at the rate of a tree sloth, I arose from bed and retreated to the easy chair. So wretched was my physical state that I wondered if it wouldn't be easier to give up the ghost.

Upon abandoning that admittedly appealing idea, it occurred to me that people are under a nearly constant state of attack by seasonal bugs. Internet research revealed that much has been written, in professional medical jargon, concerning each type of bug (insect or microbe). Still, I found no information comparing the differences involved in dealing with both life forms.

So, I reckoned that if such data were compiled in layman's words, it would offer nonprofessional victims a tool for better understanding their cyclical adversaries. Clearly, the situation cried out for a concerned citizen with vast seasonal suffering experience to craft said document. Meeting all the qualifications, I undertook the daunting project. Following are my candid notes.

To begin, there's a sharp contrast in the way in which seasonal bugs smote their targets. Typically, summer bugs (horseflies, wasps, mosquitoes, etc.) bite, sting, and make unauthorized blood withdrawals at will. However, to accomplish said deeds, they have to land on their prey. Thus, their dastardly acts are not only painful but also intrusive of one's personal space. Then again, in summer insects' defense, at least they're sporting enough to expose themselves to a bludgeoning hand.

Conversely, winter bugs (colds, flues, sore throats, etc.) are vastly more intrusive in that the infection-causing microorganisms brashly enter the sanctity of their prey's life-sustaining bloodstream. Moreover, because they are invisible, infection can be transmitted in seemingly harmless ways. For instance, the average poor slob can catch a cold simply by borrowing a sick person's handkerchief. Similarly, an unfortunate wretch can contract the flu just by strolling into the splatter pattern of a gaping mouthed, double-nostrilled, supersonic sneeze.

Another significant dissimilarity lies in the length of time a casualty suffers after a seasonal bug's assault. Sure, some summer horse fly bites knock their prey to their knees. Likewise, wasp stings inspire wildly animated reactions. In both cases, however, the symptoms last only for a short time. Then again, many winter bug infections reduce their victim's to a bedridden, fungus-like state for weeks. Worse yet, their symptoms can hang on until the return of the summer bugs and the sick cycle starts over again.

Additional differences involve the cost of overcoming a seasonal bug's attack. Although the bites of a few summer insects can transmit diseases, by and large, it's a situation of, "chomp and adios." Conversely, ridding oneself of winter bugs requires recurring doctor appointments (each accompanied by a wheelbarrow full of medications). Hence, even after a laborious recovery, victims often remain housebound because to venture out and enjoy life again would put them in the poor house.

Ultimately, my candid observations don't constitute a comprehensive study of the subject matter. However, they do expose some less-explored differences involved in dealing with seasonal bugs. Anyway, here's hoping my earnest efforts aid other sufferers in better understanding their cyclical adversaries. After all, one doesn't want to give up the ghost based on a misconception.

Famine Fare

Questioning the lofty status of "exotic" cuisine

Goodness knows I am not one to casually criticize the eating preferences of others. It would also be wrong to imply that I am a fussy eater. In fact, I have consumed some pretty bizarre victuals in my time. I refer to such delicacies as water buffalo steak, woodchuck potpie, fried jackrabbit, and breaded sucker patties. Even so, there is some supposedly exotic cuisine I know better than to consume without ever having tasted it.

For example, May 24th is National Escargot Day. I knew the dish was popular in France, but I never thought it was in such demand in the U.S. to warrant a national day of recognition. Obviously, I was wrong. Still, the unsavory truth is that escargot (French for snails) is a member of the Mollusk family of creatures, which means they are squishy invertebrates (animals without skeletons). Just touching one of the slimy, sticky, slinking organisms is enough to convince me not to insert it into my mouth, let alone chomp down on it.

Furthermore, I openly question the sanity of anyone who goes around turning over stones, looking for something to eat. Neither am I impressed with folks who dine on creatures that creep along the surface of the earth. After all, those are the sorts of primal life-forms lizards slurp up with their tongues, and what's good enough for lizards certainly isn't good enough for me. For all the above reasons, I believe, rather than being considered "exotic," escargot belongs in the culinary category of "famine fare."

While mulling over those appetite-annihilating details, I was reminded of some other dreadful indulgences which might someday attain a national day of recognition. First to come to mind was that lip-smacking, Chinese favorite, "bird's nest soup." Over time, I have inspected my share of bird dwellings. In the process, l learned that, because a bird's nest is essentially a bird's house, like humans, the feathered inhabitants use it for all their domestic needs. Hence, as I see it, making soup out of a bird's nest is akin to boiling a well-patronized, kitty litter box. Be still my foolish gut.

Equally appalling, the Chinese also eat eggs that were purposefully buried in the ground several months previous. Obviously, the question begs, why would anyone put a raw egg into a hole, bury it, and then allow the egg to putrefy, before digging it up again and devouring it? Personally, rather than partake of such killer-cuisine, I'd prefer to scour the bottom of a ripe dumpster with a Shop-vac to procure my lunch.

Lastly, there's that celebrated eastern-European delicacy, "caviar." In reality, the supposedly luxurious entre is nothing more than a glob of pickled sturgeon roe (aka fish eggs). To be certain, I have used cured fish eggs as bait to catch other fish. On the other hand, I like to think that, as a human being, my culinary preferences should be slightly more sophisticated than those of a gilled creature. Furthermore, to my discriminating eye, caviar resembles tar pit oozings daubed on a wafer. Someone hold me back.

Ultimately, in an attempt to demote snails to their rightful status as—famine fare, I am prepared to champion the repeal of National Escargot Day. After all, allowing escargot to maintain its current lofty designation leaves the door open for National Birds'-Nest Soup Day, National Buried Egg Day and National Caviar Day. What's next? National Jelly Fish Jam Day? Yum-Yum.

A Few Issues

Some thoughts on the art of venting gracefully

Heaven knows I don't complain easily. However, over time, it is nigh onto impossible not to compile a list of issues. That is not to confuse "issues" with the multitude of petty grievances that attend every life. Rather, I refer to those events which leave a residue of indignation in the mind. When enough of said residue compiles, it inevitably turns sour. At that moment, as I see it, a person has two choices: "go nuts" or "vent." Given that from day-to-day, my sanity is already questionable, I choose the latter.

Still, there are rules of acceptable venting. For instance, any insensitive brute can brashly vocalize his or her mega-frustrations in a public setting. In fact, a rash of such unsightly, noisy spectacles has occurred in the Tri-cities urban area recently. Thus, for the sake of community civility, I feel obliged to demonstrate the less clamorous, written method of expressing personal outrage. Ensuing are some illustrations.

For decades, every morning, I devotedly scalded the inside of my mouth with Listerine mouthwash. Convinced that, as advertised, all the germs in my mouth would be eradicated, I gargled until my mouth felt as though it would catch fire. Only to find out recently that in all that time, I never killed a dad-blamed thing. In fact, my halitosis not only survived but thrived. By any measure of justice, a man should be able to sue.

For years I sent a color photograph of myself to my friends and relatives as Christmas presents. Naturally, folks treasured my thoughtful, unique gifts. Indeed, many were so emotionally overcome they forgot to send a thank-you card. Regrettably, that time-honored tradition is presently in grave peril. In what I suspect is a devious reference to my advancing years, my color-photo printer has taken to printing all color pictures of me in black and white only. Consequently, my once stately image has been transformed into that of a Prohibition-Era mobster. Unbelievable as it may seem, I suspect foul play from a familial source.

Another of my persistent peeves involves the decline of common courtesy. As a case in point, recently while eating breakfast at the cafe in Harrison, I engaged in conversation with a customer of roughly my age. When I casually mentioned that my back was a little sore, the insensitive oaf had the audacity to interrupt with, "Heck, that ain't nothin." He then proceeded to boisterously recite a long list of his own aches and pains. Shocked speechless, I squeezed a plastic jug of maple syrup so hard, its contents squirted onto the ceiling. Talk about rude! Any redneck knows it's an inexcusable breach of etiquette to interrupt a man before he's finished sniveling.

There, I feel better now. My sanity is semi-secure—for a while. My feelings of injustice have been soothed. Better yet, no innocent bystanders had to endure the vocal ranting of another person. As shown above, venting issues silently on paper may offer a higher path. With any luck, local residue removers will adopt this "art of venting gracefully." Only then will our Tri-cities' civility be restored. Even better, folks might recall that there's more to be happy about than to be upset over.

Now, if I can just get the color-printer working again before Christmas.

A Quest for Clarity

Dealing with maddening misnomers

Last night, I woke up in the middle of the night with my mind racing. For the rest of the night, I tossed and turned in mental tempest. What was the cause of my discontent? In the midst of slumber, inexplicably, the word "butterfly" flashed through my mind. Surely, to the great majority of folks, such an occurrence would have been no big deal. However, zealot for linguistic clarity that I am, I couldn't ignore the fact that, as I see it, the word butterfly is a blatant example of a "misnomer."

According to the Free Online Dictionary, a misnomer is "an incorrect or unsuitable name or term for a person or thing." Simply put, it means that someone or something has been misnamed.

Continuing that line of thought, I can honestly say, I have yet to encounter a quarter-pound of butter flying around our local meadows. However, in those same meadows, numerous caterpillar-derived, winged insects have fluttered past me that matched the dictionary's definition of a butterfly. Hence, the maddening question begs, "Why wasn't the butterfly dubbed the 'flutterby?'"

Given the abundance of self-appointed, English-usage police, one would think that such a clearly misleading name would have been brought to light long before. Such has not been the case. Hence, I have selflessly taken it upon myself to boldly step up to the keyboard and launch a quest for linguistic clarity. Following is an initial list of maddening misnomers, plus my clarified, alternative terms:

- Hay fever - not caused by hay nor is it a fever =

"seasonal spastic schnoz syndrome"

- Cow pie - not meant for consumption, but spurs plant growth = "cow compost cluster"
- Pronghorn antelope - not an antelope, but a species of goat = "pronghorn galloping goat"
- Mountain goat - not a goat, but a species of antelope = "ashen alpine antelope"
- Prairie dog - not a canine, but a rodent = "range rat"
- Groundhog - not a pig, but a ground squirrel = "supersized subterranean squirrel"
- Hunting rifle - a rifle never hunted anything = "hunter's howitzer"
- Brook trout - not a trout, but a species of arctic char = "cold creek char"
- Robin - actually a thrush = "blush-breasted thrush"
- Horse fly - bites people too = "big, biting, butt-ugly bug"
- Funny bone - not funny nor is it a bone = "unnerving nerve ending"
- Black ice - not black but clear (aka invisible) = "black and blue butt ice"

Below are additional misnomers encountered in daily life plus my clarified alternative terms.

- Multitasking - more accurately = "simultaneous shoddy overtasking"
- Bipartisan legislation - extinct congressional procedure = "limbo law"
- Political dialogue - juvenile at best = "taxpayer-subsidized name-calling"
- Outsourcing - call a spade a spade = "jobflushing"
- Credit card - let's get real = "stratospheric-interest debt card"

- E-mail - carrier pigeon is safer = “easily-monitored virus-conduit”
- Alarm clock - no need for shock = “depraved, dream-destroying device”
- Coffee - more descriptive = “starter solution”
- Doughnut - not a nut, but circular = “doughring”

In the end, there’s no denying, the English language is in a constant state of transformation. Therefore, as quickly as I identify maddening misnomers, new examples are added. Alas, my selfless quest for clarity goes on, one sleepless night at a time.

Weigh Day

How to make performing a critical event less grueling

As a young man, I only weighed myself when I thought I didn't weigh enough. Oh how things have changed with time. Nowadays, once a month, I force myself to endure what I call, "Weigh Day." Weigh Day consists of the following subsections: the "Day before Weigh Day," the "Morning of Total Tonnage Tally," the "Scale Compression Session," and the "Scale Confession Session."

Fortunately, over the years, I have also developed a course of action designed to tip the balance (no pun intended) in a man's favor on Weigh Day. So, in order to reach out to fellow ever-blossoming-butt sufferers, I have decided to share my procedures, in sequential order.

Day before Weigh Day

- Begin fasting at dawn.
- Go to a barbershop and get your hair cropped short.
- Have the barber trim your eyebrows and remove the hair on the ears and the back of your neck.
- Use a pre-colonoscopy-like purgative to eliminate all solids from the innards.
- Thoroughly scrub the bathroom scale to remove any traces of dirt, dust, or toe jam.

Morning of Total Tonnage Tally

- Continue fasting.
- Unburden the body of weighty interior liquids.
- Remove contact lenses.
- Use tweezers to extract hefty navel lint.

- Shower twice using a scouring pad and lye soap.
- Set the shower head to "high pressure jet" mode, and scour the ears of bulky wax buildup.
- Dry off with a leaf blower.
- Shave your face four ways (up, down, left to right, right to left) with a new 4-bladed razor.
- Trim your toe and finger nails to the meat.
- Floss the teeth thoroughly with sticky dental floss to remove compacted, beefy food particles.
- Brush your teeth (front, back and top) with a high-speed, multi-directional, electric tooth brush.
- Gargle vigorously with bacteria-killing mouth wash in three repetitions.
- Blow-dry the inside of the mouth (including beneath the tongue) to remove all moisture.
- Blow-dry your hair until it begins to smolder.
- Be careful not to apply any weighty deodorant or aftershave.
- Forcefully, blow the nose until it makes a dry, honking sound.

Scale Compression Session

- Take a deep breath and exhale all the air from the lungs.
- Gently mount the bathroom scale with both heels positioned at the far rear of the scale.
- With one eye open, look down.

The Dreaded Scale Confession Session

- Visually note the recorded weight.
- Step off the bathroom scale before turning purple and exhale.
- Verbally confess your true weight.

- Try not to wail so loud as to alarm the neighbors.

On a final note, perhaps the best idea would be to purchase a metric scale and destroy any accompanying conversion tables. After all, Weigh Day is an example of when ignorance truly is bliss. Besides, confession may be good for the soul, but it can also be bad for one's self-esteem.

Reverse-time-travel

Adjusting to life without a personal computer

Recently, I was Internet researching some material for a writing piece when, abruptly, the mouse pointer became immobile and none of the keyboard keys were functional. Just like that, my computer was locked up. Consequently, I was forced to shut it down by unplugging the power cord from the wall outlet. Five interminable minutes later, I swallowed hard, restarted the cherished machine and nervously waited for the desktop to reload. Unfortunately, early in the loading process, an ominous error message appeared on the monitor screen informing me that my personal computer (PC) was out of action.

Within an hour, my ailing Central Processing Unit (CPU) and I were at a computer repair shop. Upon entering, I sensed that, based on my "so last century" appearance, the young man at the counter had already judged me as being "technologically-impaired." Nevertheless, he listened politely to my tale of web woe. Then, in the compassionless monotone tech-geeks are notorious for, he provided three gut-wrenching scenarios: 1) my PC might not be repairable, 2) I might need to purchase a new (expensive) machine, and most distressing, 3) my current files might not be recoverable to install on the new model. Only further detailed assessment would reveal the actual circumstances.

Suddenly, I was confronted with the horrendous fact that, for the first time in twenty years, I was temporarily going to have to adjust to life without a personal computer. Immediately, images of looming submission-due-dates and unfinished articles began flashing in my mind. Just then, I had to fight off the urge to bury a nearby ink pen in my jugular vein.

Back home, in desperation, I tried writing a newspaper article by hand. It didn't take long to realize my penmanship had devolved into indecipherable scribble. It was then I remembered why I bought a computer with word processing capabilities in the first place: "No matter how measly one's words-per-minute count, it's difficult to type illegibly."

Having accepted the fact my writing would have to wait, I focused on remembering what I used to do with my time before I owned a computer. As a result, I took road trips to Ringling and Radersburg just so folks there could get to see me. My brother and I went fishing, thereby reigniting a festering sibling competition. I drove into the local mountains where, inspired by the autumn scenery, I contemplated profound philosophical concepts such as, "If a tree falls in a forest, and no one is around to hear it, does anybody really care if it makes noise?"

Back home again, I found myself staring at the empty space where my CPU usually resided. While so doing, I realized I couldn't access the world-wide-web from the privacy of my home. Surprisingly, I also took comfort in the fact that neither could the world-wide-web access the privacy of my home. Nevertheless, the aforementioned publication deadlines still had to be met and the articles emailed to publishers. With that sobering thought, my experiment in reverse-time-travel ended.

Finally, I recalled that the local public school had both computers and Internet access. A telephone call resulted in an invitation to use said equipment. Thus, thanks to their generosity, I will survive without my PC until I get it back. Nonetheless, there's no denying, my brief experiment in reverse time travel proved to be enormously enjoyable.

Management Material

The story of a supervisory debut gone bad

During the early 1990s, I worked as a heavy-equipment operator at an open-pit talc mine south of Ennis. One day, the foreman asked for a volunteer to fill in for him when he wasn't able to make it to work. As luck would have it, I'd been waiting anxiously for just such an opportunity to display my hitherto unacknowledged supervisory ability. So, I volunteered. A month later, the foreman called in sick. At last, my momentous managerial debut had arrived.

To begin, I professionally lined the crew out and got work under way. Then, two hours into the shift, I needed to discuss something with the bulldozer operator. So, I drove from the open-pit mining area down to where he was pushing waste rock near the maintenance shop and called him on the mobile radio. When he answered, I asked Marley (not his actual name) to back up to where I was standing (about seventy-five yards behind him) and stop.

While in the process of backing up, Marley remarked, "Art, I can't see you." So, to make myself more conspicuous, I waved my hard hat overhead. Then, while still a distance off, the dozer stopped. At last, I reckoned he'd seen me. On the contrary, the old boy announced, "Sorry, but I've yet to lay eyes on you." Frustrated by then, I began to jump up and down and flail my right arm, while shouting into the radio, "What are you, blind? I'm right over here." Interminable seconds later, Marley replied with equal frustration, "Well I must be blind because I sure as blazes don't see you."

When the dozer resumed pushing rock again a light came

on in the murky recesses of my brain. I abruptly remembered I had taken Marley out of the dozer earlier to run the fuel truck in the mining area and had replaced him with another dozer operator. Hence, the hard-at-work man in the dozer still had no idea he was the object of a contentious conversation while, a half-mile away, Marley was feverishly backing the fuel truck around the open-pit area, searching for a phantom foreman.

With Marley impatiently awaiting a reply, I desperately searched for a plausible explanation that wouldn't make me sound like a complete idiot. When none was forthcoming, I panicked and blurted out the humiliating facts as they were. That's when events took a dramatic turn for the worse.

There are no words to describe the dread that engulfed me when I came to grips with the fact that the entire mortifying dialogue had just been broadcast to gleeful ears across the whole property. Consequently, my radio fairly erupted with less than complimentary, cutting remarks. Even worse, the mine superintendent, who was driving home in a company vehicle at the time, also overheard every scintillating syllable. So, he too called on his radio to inform me that he laughed so hard he had to pull off the road to regain his composure. The final indignity came later when the boss revealed that, during that time, he had thought to himself, "Now there's a prime example of management material if ever there was one."

In the end, my eagerly-awaited supervisory debut proved to be a debacle. Amazingly enough, after that exemplary exhibition of incompetence, I was still allowed to fill in for the foreman. I think it was only because everyone was hoping I would top my inaugural performance. Thankfully, I didn't.

New-New Year's Resolutions

Some thoughts on a different method of achieving annual goals

Like many folks, I have faithfully set New Year's resolutions, for as long as I can remember. Unfortunately, primarily because achieving resolutions involves resolve, my record of keeping those goals is not sterling. It's not that I don't possess resolve, it's just that it tends to dissolve rather quickly. After so many years of failing to reach my annual goals, I am beginning to lose faith in myself. Obviously, such a state of mind can be detrimental to one's self-image. As a result, this year I have decided to enhance my odds of success by crafting goals that are slightly less challenging. For instance, as self-improvement goals, I pledge to:

- Evolve
- Limit television viewing time to no longer than I am awake
- Do more laundry, use less deodorant
- Grow older
- Consume more fruit and vegetables occasionally
- Sleep less, nap more
- Procrastinate less when I have time
- Exercise more, exert less
- Spend less time on my home computer when the power is off
- Grow more gray whiskers
- Only answer my phone when it rings
- Eat less, but more often

Of course, my social skills always require improvement-oriented resolutions. Hence, I swear to:

- Not offend more people than I embarrass
- Not deliberately turn off my hearing aid while someone is talking to me
- Listen closely, from afar
- Argue less frequently by disregarding other's opinions
- Shout less, rant more
- Quit saying, "just sayin"
- Impart less unsolicited advice while offering more helpful suggestions
- Wait until a person has finished sniveling before telling him/her about my problems
- Avoid yawning while listening to someone's harrowing tale of survival
- Suffer in dignified silence while being ignored in deafening silence

Lastly, as pertains to my writing, I vow to:

- Type faster, but with more mistakes
- Concentrate on effective use of language and the blazes with grammar
- Limit use of the term "bless your butt"
- Only write abstractly (dazzle with BS) when I can't express what I am trying to describe literally
- Don't never use no triple negatives
- Never eat sauerkraut and Polish sausage before a public reading
- Not write in a voice that's overly serious

By this time next year, through minimal effort, measly resolve and shrewdly chosen goals, I will have fulfilled my new-New Year's resolutions. Consequently, my self-image will have been renovated to its former state of mediocrity. Who knows? My avant-garde method might even spur a goal-setting trend.

Modern Writers' Relaxation Routine

Suggestions on preparing to write

Recently, while working on a piece of creative literature, I was reminded that writing requires exertion. Thus, I reasoned that every composition endeavor should be preceded by a relaxation program to properly prime the writer for his or her work. As I thought about it, I realized that relaxation methods such as yoga and meditation employ ambiguous, one-method-fits-all strategies when, in fact, writers are an undeniably unique breed. Like a jeweler striving to cut a diamond, writers spend endless hours in solitude, resolutely sorting words. Accordingly, my revolutionary routine takes place on-site, in that quasi-mystical composition setting variously known as: "the author's asylum," "the creative cave," "hallucination hermitage," or "the word nerd's world."

Additionally, today's authors often prefer to use computers instead of traditional pen and paper. Thus, the situation also cried out for relaxation tactics specifically tailored for modern writers. With those facts in mind, after vigorous brainstorming, my detailed and innovative pre-writing relaxation methodology emerged as follows.

Upon reaching the writing destination, be seated and address the computer. Take three deep breaths and exhale fully. Place your reading glasses on the toes of the left foot and your empty coffee cup over the toes of the right foot. Next, to reduce the onset of drowsiness, fully extend the legs horizontally at 90-degree angles from the body and hold.

Now carefully wedge the nose between the "B" and "N" keys on the central, lower edge of the keyboard. Release the neck muscles. As the letters of the alphabet become physically etched into the forehead, allow streaming video of words to saturate the farthest reaches of your eccentric mind. Then, download from the mind's memory cache lobe any damning dangling participles, awkward syntax, and improper grammar to the brain stem's trash bin. Lastly, exhale deeply while delicately extracting your now misshapen snout from the keyboard.

Then, embrace the Central Processing Unit (CPU) tower with both arms, and squeeze hell out of it, as you would a long-lost lover. Then, as scintillatingly descriptive phrases are saved to the life-sustaining muscle's clipboard, picture your fluttering heart and the computer's motherboard as intertwined.

Release the CPU and allow the eyes to stare longingly at the monitor screen. In the mind's eye, imagine creative ideas in rage impact font and graphic images miraculously forming on the screen. Zoom the bedazzled eyeballs into the screen itself, linking the physical with virtual reality. Then, in an interlude from the paranormal, wiggle the toes, thus restoring circulation to the legs.

Next, balance the computer screen's navigating mouse on the tip of the index finger of your dominate hand. Fully comprehend that the fate of words, paragraphs and entire chapters ride on a mere click of your omnipotent extremity upon the mouse. Audibly repeat the following adage three times: "To save or not to save, that is the question? Whether tis nobler in the grammar check to suffer the slings and arrows of outrageous critique or to take cursor, and by opposing, end them."

Lastly, lower the legs to the floor. Feel every bodily muscle crash to a jellied mass. Discharge any pent up writing block with a hearty gerund. Remove the reading glasses and coffee cup from the toes. The body is wholly relaxed and revitalized. The mind is serene yet filled with expectant words. The senses are agape. Place the trembling fingertips on the keys. Commence typing.

With all due modesty, I dare say my humble efforts may well set a new paradigm in modern writer's relaxation routines. Only time will tell.